Theodore Roosevelt

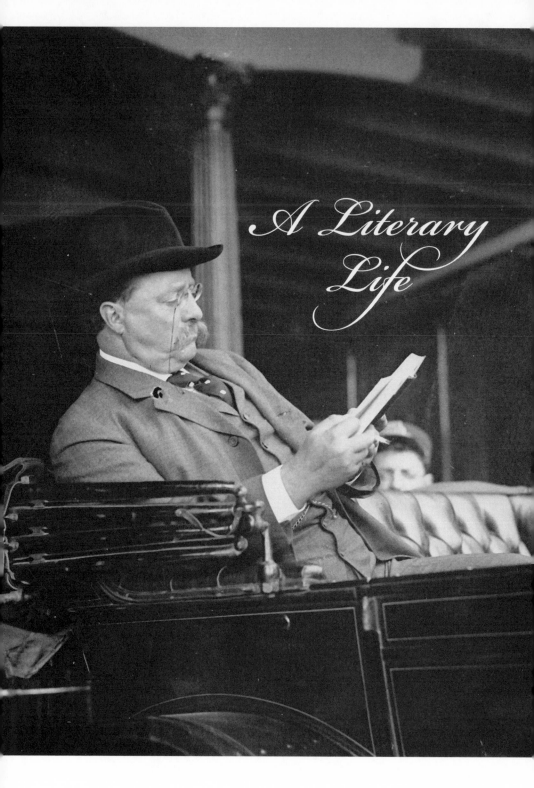

A Literary
Life

Theodore Roosevelt

THOMAS BAILEY

& KATHERINE JOSLIN

{ ForeEdge }

ForeEdge

An imprint of University Press of New England

www.upne.com

© 2018 Thomas Bailey and Katherine Joslin

Manufactured in the United States of America

Designed by Eric M. Brooks

Typeset in Monticello by Passumpsic Publishing

FRONTISPIECE: Theodore Roosevelt, at his ease, reading
in an open automobile. *Roosevelt 560.6.C71-050 olvwork382651.*
Houghton Library, Harvard University.

Library of Congress Cataloging-in-Publication Data

NAMES: Bailey, Thomas, author. | Joslin, Katherine, 1947– author.

TITLE: Theodore Roosevelt: a literary life /
Thomas Bailey and Katherine Joslin.

DESCRIPTION: Lebanon NH: ForeEdge, 2018. |
Includes bibliographical references and index.

IDENTIFIERS: LCCN 2017043420 (print) | LCCN 2017043891
(ebook) | ISBN 9781512602593 (epub, mobi, & pdf) |
ISBN 9781512601664 (cloth)

SUBJECTS: LCSH: Roosevelt, Theodore, 1858–1919 –
Writing skill. | Presidents – United States – Biography. |
English language – 19th century – Style. |
English language – 20th century – Style.

CLASSIFICATION: LCC E757 (ebook) |
LCC E757 .B17 2018 (print) | DDC 973.91/1092 [B] – dc23

LC record available at https://lccn.loc.gov/2017043420

5 4 3 2 1

To
Sally
and Jim,
and J. R.
and Mary

CONTENTS

Illustrations follow page 148

ACKNOWLEDGMENTS

We have worked together over many years and are grateful for the support of institutions and the interest of friends as our book has come into being. Western Michigan University provided Katherine a Faculty Research and Creative Activities Award as well as sabbatical leave that allowed time for scholarly work at the Houghton Library at Harvard University, and at the Library of Congress. The Eccles Centre awarded her a US Fellowship in North American Studies that opened up archives in the British Library.

Early in our research, we were lucky to have the advice of Wallace Finley Dailey, then the curator of the Theodore Roosevelt Collection at Harvard. We add our thanks to those of other Roosevelt scholars over the past forty years who have benefited from Wallace's unfailing expertise and unflagging enthusiasm. We are grateful to his successor Heather Cole and to Pamela Pierce, archivist at the Theodore Roosevelt Center at Dickinson Sate University, for good advice along the way. For generous help, we also thank Mary LeCroy at the American Museum of Natural History, Susan Sarna at Sagamore Hill National Historic Site, Nancy Malloy, archivist at the American Academy of Arts and Letters, and the staffs at the Royal Geographical Society Archives in London and at Bulloch Hall in Roswell, Georgia.

We are grateful to Philip Davies, director of the Eccles Center for American Studies, and his knowledgeable staff in the British Library who led us beyond American shores to think of Roosevelt in the international arena. At the University of Liverpool, we are grateful to fellow Edith Wharton scholar Janet Beer, who is vice chancellor, and her colleague David Seed, for supporting our work on Roosevelt. In England, too, we thank Avril Horner for advice on writing biography, and we are always delighted with the insights of David Woodman and Howard Horner.

Friend and colleague Shirley Clay Scott, former Ruth and Harold Newman Dean of the School of Arts and Sciences at Hunter College, has been steadfast in her support of this project from its very beginning, reading draft after draft, offering invaluable advice, and joining us for an occasional Manhattan. Her colleague Charles Fanning, professor emeritus of history and English at Southern Illinois University, graciously gave us a useful reading of chapters. Carl Smith, professor emeritus of English at Northwestern University, encouraged and advised us as the manuscript grew into a book. Jax Gardiner was an expert research assistant, Rebecca Siegel built a smart and useful index, Glenn Novak worked hard to catch our errors in his copyediting, and Colleen Woolpert made us look good in the photograph. We thank them all.

At the Theodore Roosevelt Symposium in Dickinson, North Dakota, in September 2017, we made the acquaintance of Clay Jenkinson, Sharon Kilzer, Char Miller, Darrin Lunde, and other scholars who are doing fresh and engaging work on Theodore Roosevelt. We wish we'd had access in particular to Darrin Lunde's fine book, *The Naturalist: Theodore Roosevelt, a Lifetime of Exploration, and The Triumph of American Natural History* as we were writing this one.

At the University Press of New England, we have been fortunate to have the knowledge and exuberance of our editor Richard Pult, who admitted he is a pushover for Theodore Roosevelt. UPNE is a wonderful place, full of smart and skilled people dedicated to the crafting of books. We are pleased to be publishing with them.

Our yoga friends, Vaughn and Jan Maatman, Kevin Corder and Susan Hoffmann, Brian Wilson and Cybelle Shattuck, and Diana Wilson, seem not to have tired in talking about Theodore Roosevelt. We thank them. Over the long years, we are grateful for good friends with true interest in our writing project; in Michigan, Irma López and Ben Jones; in Vermont, Laurie and Herb Ferris, Michael Maddalena and Rebecca Siegel; and in California, our late friend Jon Strolle, and Barbara and Mel Liner.

Close to home, we thank our children, Cullen and Mike, Kate, Sam, Emily and Jon, and their children, Emily and Dave, Maggie, Clem, Elli, Tom, Cat, and Ivan Rex, and even another generation, Emmet James. Theodore Roosevelt would be proud of such kids; certainly we are.

As our book comes into its own life, we are grateful to be married still and, even, to like each other.

Theodore Roosevelt

An American-American Writer

> The tragedy of Roosevelt seems to me to lie in this: That he
> was a man of remarkable literary talent who is known chiefly for his
> politics. . . . Roosevelt bore the hallmark of a genuine man of letters
> and, had he devoted his life altogether to composition, he would have
> gained for himself a position in American literature equaled by
> few other men. . . . Roosevelt slung a wicked pen.
> { Charles W. Ferguson, "Roosevelt — Man of Letters," 1927 }[1]

> I have always had a horror of words that are not translated
> into deeds, of speech that does not result in action — in other words,
> I believe in realizable ideals and in realizing them, in preaching
> what can be practiced and then in practicing it.
> { Theodore Roosevelt, *An Autobiography*, 1913 }[2]

Theodore Roosevelt could not stop writing, just as he could not stop talking and as he could not stop reading, the world he saw and heard flowing through him into language, pages and pages of prose. From the time he first scrawled his baby name "Tedie" (simplifying the spelling of Teedie) with a pencil, he wrote every day, often for much of the day, in letters and journals and field books, illustrated with sketches, and later, as he matured, he considered himself a literary man and worked hard to turn his experiments with language into art and income.[3] Henry Adams famously dubbed Roosevelt "pure act" and dismissed him as a thinker and a writer, and yet, for Roosevelt, thinking *was* action, and the use of language *was* pure act. He made little distinction between thinking and saying or saying and writing or between writing and doing; writing for him was "the strenuous life," the writer always in the "sweat and dust" of "the arena." Over the course of his long and productive life, he seldom said a word that he or someone else didn't write down.

In striking ways, his life in language was a monologue written in the moment or, soon after, in reflections that mimicked the moment, giving him as a writer a series of direct, seemingly honest glimpses of the world around him. His childhood writing came so rapidly that at times he drew symbols in the prose line and made maps and sketches to orient his reader, whoever that reader might have been. He began journal entries with a list of characters, as though he were writing a play: "When I put 'we 3' I mean Ellie Conie and I. When I put 'big people' I mean Papa Mama and Bamie." Ellie was his younger brother Elliott, Conie his baby sister Corinne, and Bamie his older sister Anna.[4] He even listed himself as the author: "Journal of Theodore Roosevelt of U.S.A. New York." The journals were clearly not for his eyes only, rarely confessional or intimate, and the boy seemed not to have had his family in mind as readers. Tedie, even in these earliest of literary experiments, narrated his life to an outside reader, in some way for posterity, perhaps for us. In that spirit, we come to read him. Later in life, as he worked to meet publication deadlines for a wider audience, he packed a camera to capture images that the pen could not record as quickly as he moved, or to prove that his pen was telling the truth.

Tedie and his siblings were raised by parents who believed that education comes from genuine experience and had the money to provide years of travel and time for exploration of the wider world. The Roosevelt household was full of books. Free from the usual routines of American education, the children read novels and histories and poems of all sorts. Aloysius A. Norton, TR's first literary biographer, pointed out that Theodore Sr. raised his children as he had been schooled, sending the boys for a time to his mentor John McMullen, who believed in a liberal education focused on transcendental notions of individualism, buffered by honesty and directness to "eliminate false pretentions and vanity."[5] Tedie's asthma often kept him at home, where Aunt Anna Bulloch Gracie, his mother's sister, taught the children how to read and write, and where later his sister Anna watched over his studies.

The boy read without prejudice or squeamishness. He adored the poems of Henry Wadsworth Longfellow, the novels of Sir Walter Scott and Charles Dickens, and the sea stories of Frederick Marryat, along with tales intended for girls, including Harriet Beecher Stowe's *Little Pussy Willow* (1870), which begins: "I hope that you will all grow up to be nice good girls like her, with bright, healthy faces, and cheerful hearts, and the gift of always seeing *The Bright Side of Everything*."[6] Tedie enjoyed Adeline Dutton Train Whitney's *A Summer in Leslie Goldthwaite's Life*,

Louisa May Alcott's *An Old-Fashioned Girl*, and Louise Ouida's *Under Two Flags* (a book that would surface in his own later writing).[7] The Roosevelts subscribed to *Our Young Folks, an Illustrated Magazine for Boys and Girls*, which may well have introduced the Roosevelt children to writers who would become favorites, including Alcott, Longfellow, Stowe, and Mayne Reid.[8] Dime novels, however, were taboo by Mother's edict, and thus Tedie surreptitiously read any he could get his hands on and would binge on "cheap fiction" all his life. During the family tours of Europe, he read Reid's adventure novels, along with the popular natural histories of John George Wood and the birding stories of John James Audubon, bundles of such books always accompanying the Roosevelt children. "I suppose we have read 50 since we left America," he reported in his diary after four weeks in Europe.[9] As a teenager, Theodore caught up on conventional studies at the Arthur Cutler School in New York in order to bring his academic training into line with what Harvard expected its young men to know as they entered college. Throughout his life, he never spent a day without a book in hand or in close reach, picking it up as respite from play or as reprieve from boredom or duty, filling each moment with language.

From his first tentative days with a pen at seven years old until his death at sixty, Roosevelt crafted language in many moods, at times lyrical and impressionistic, and at other times sober and scientific, and often, especially in later life, didactic and obdurate. He meant to be taken seriously and hoped to claim for himself a reputation as, what he quipped only slightly in jest, an "American-American" writer. His prose style is clear if not elegant, with a loose and repetitive structure that follows the sound of the American voice. The voices of Benjamin Franklin, Ralph Waldo Emerson, Henry David Thoreau, Walt Whitman, John Burroughs, Jane Addams, Edith Wharton, and Booker T. Washington all come to mind in thinking about the prose style of Theodore Roosevelt.

His literary range was wide within the confines of nonfiction prose as he mastered the art of writing journals, narratives, essays, speeches, books, and letters. Toward the end of his life, he boasted that he had written as many as 150,000 letters, from which Massachusetts Institute of Technology professor Elting E. Morison, as head of the Theodore Roosevelt Research Project, culled an eight-volume selection.[10] Collections of his letters, one recently assembled by Henry William Brands, tell stories worthy of any good novel because his writing was at its most vivid and witty when he was talking directly to someone he knew.[11] During Roosevelt's lifetime, his essays and narrative sketches appeared in all sorts of magazines, including the *Outing Magazine, Forest and Stream, Century*, the *Atlantic Monthly, Cosmopolitan*, the *Independent*, the *Bookman*, the *Ladies' Home Journal*, and the *Outlook*, where he had an office in later years as a contributing editor. British reviewers in the *Times* thought of him as a journalist because he placed his early articles in popular magazines, before collecting them into books, a process that allowed him to earn money in one venue and again in another. All his life, he would look for ways to restate, rewrite, and repackage his prose, pushing nearly every single word into print.

Roosevelt crafted political speeches, hundreds of them, reading or reciting them at rallies large and small, and then weaving them into editorials and essays, many of them cobbled together into his books on statecraft. William Draper Lewis recalled an evening before a speech in Carnegie Hall on March 20, 1912, when in his "low-ceilinged study" at Sagamore Hill, Roosevelt kept his Progressive Party friend up past midnight, emphatically reading lines from a long manuscript, some pages typed and others scrawled in pencil on soiled tissue paper. "What he wanted was not to be told what to say, but to be helped how to say it," Lewis noted.[12] Clear in Roosevelt's mind was that the text he was crafting would be published in the morning newspapers before journalists weighed in on what they may have heard him say. He is best known today for the strident notes of his political prose, the sort of language he believed Americans wanted to hear from a leader, most especially from a president.

In various moods, Roosevelt turned his mind to writing about science and history, adventure and travel, as well as the personal delights of work and play. Harvard University professor Hermann Hagedorn, who became friends with Roosevelt in his last months, did more than any scholar to preserve and promote his literary voice in establishing the Roosevelt Memorial Association (chartered by an act of Congress on May 31, 1920, and renamed the Theodore Roosevelt Association in 1953) and edited the Memorial Edition of *The Works of Theodore Roosevelt* in twenty-four volumes.[13] The Houghton and Widener Libraries at Harvard University house a collection of his childhood writing and family correspondence, given by the Roosevelt Memorial Association in 1943. Roosevelt reigned in the years before presidential libraries became the norm, and he and his wife Edith Carow Roosevelt gave his presidential papers to the Library of Congress, where during the 1960s' Presidential Papers Project they were preserved on 485 reels of microfilm that today are being digitized, together with the Houghton manuscripts and others, by the Theodore Roosevelt Center at Dickinson State University, whose goal is to create a virtual archive, online and accessible to everybody, as well as to build the Theodore Roosevelt Presidential Library in North Dakota. The Theodore Roosevelt Almanac, too, offers online links to documents that define his various political and social roles—President, Politician, Soldier, Author, Outdoorsman, and Family—following a pattern set by the University of Chicago English professor Edward Wagenknecht in *The Seven Worlds of Theodore Roosevelt* (1958), dividing his life into categories—Action, Thought, Human Relations, Family, Spiritual Values, Public Affairs, and War and Peace.[14] An astonishing array of texts is online in various and curious places, a cache that offers fresh ways to read what he had to say.

Roosevelt thought himself a literary man by the time he was thirty, publishing three books in 1888 that signaled the scope and variety of his prose: *Essays on Practical Politics*, a book made up of two seminal essays on governmental reform; *Gouverneur Morris*, the second of his academic histories about political life in America; and, closer to his heart, *Ranch Life and the Hunting-Trail*, a second book about his life in the natural world. With those early successes in three distinct fields of writing, he wrote Jonas S. Van Duzer, a former colleague in the New York State Legislature, a reflective letter about his chances in life. "Like yourself, I shall probably never be in politics again," Roosevelt began; he had been elected to the state legislature in 1882, 1883, and 1884, but had been bruised politically in a losing bid for mayor of New York City in 1886. And then Roosevelt turned an equally cold eye on his prospects as a writer: "My literary work occupies a good deal of my time; and I have on the whole done fairly well at it; I should like to write some book that would really rank as in the very first class, but I suppose this is a mere dream."[15] Had he never become president of the United States, he might well be remembered as a literary man among those in the first class of American writers.

He believed in wide-ranging study of history, philosophy, science, and, most especially, imaginative literature. Even as academic education around him was fragmenting into specialized disciplines, he sought ways of bringing fields of study together. Take the hunting tale, for example. "The hunting book proper," he argued in a 1911 column for the *Outlook*, "goes back at least to Xenophon."[16] Back, that is to say, to the Greeks, and he knew that from his early studies of the Greek language. Xenophon, a contemporary of Plato and student of Socrates, wrote in a relatively readable style, simple and direct, the sort of style that even a poor student in classical languages could manage. Theodore had asked his sister Anna to send him his copy of Xenophon during his freshmen year at Harvard, even as Greek was earning his lowest grade. Xenophon's military memoirs, long histories, and, especially, tales of hunting and farming appealed to the young man, who would come to write in all these literary genres. His moral philosophy, too, would come to look much like Xenophon's, based on self-control, the ethic of work, the ideal of service, and a strong belief in utilitarianism and egalitarianism. Xenophon's "On Hunting" was the very sort of prose model that the young Harvard student was searching for. In later life, he argued that a thinker like Xenophon, schooled in many disciplines and thinking across them all, was hard to find in the modern stratified world. "The nature book proper, which treats with power and charm of outdoor life," he cautioned, could not come from a mind steeped in only one field of study. The best writing comes "from the standpoint, not of the mere hunter or mere zoologist, but of the man of letters and learning who is in love with nature." He credited John Burroughs with being the "highest expression" of the nature writer in American literature.

By 1912, Roosevelt's work as a historian earned him the presidency of the American Historical Association, and from that bully pulpit he delivered a signature address, "History as Literature," about the literary nature of all good writing. One stunning example for him was evolution. Scientists in the nineteenth century had "grasped the fact of evolution," he noted. "Yet, where their predecessors had created hardly a ripple, Darwin and Huxley succeeded in effecting a complete revolution in the thought of the age."[17] That revolution in thought came precisely because "what Darwin and Huxley wrote was interesting to read." Collections of data and specialized treatises may be useful but will not be read for long, he warned writers of all sorts. "The great speeches of statesmen and the great writings of historians can live only if they possess the deathless quality that inheres in all great literature," he thundered. A real writer has "the power to embody ghosts, to put flesh and blood on dry bones, to make dead men live before our eyes."[18]

The question for the young Roosevelt was whether he could bring his own writing to vivid life, and his early reviewers, most of them humanities professors, took his literary measure. William Peterfield Trent, professor of English literature at Columbia University, reviewed Roosevelt's *The Winning of the West*, praising his ability to bring the past into relevance with the present and his characters to life; but Professor Trent kept his red pen in hand. "When he is at his best, Mr. Roosevelt writes as well as any man need desire to write," he conceded, adding the caveat, "who is not aiming at that elusive glory of being considered a master of style."[19] The apprentice writer's style "not infrequently shows traces of hurry," the professor chided, and he often writes too much. That is not to say that Roosevelt wasn't aiming for "elusive glory."

"Roosevelt slung a wicked pen," declared the literary critic Charles W. Ferguson in a 1927 retrospective, "Roosevelt—Man of Letters," marking the publication of the National Edition of *The Works of Theodore Roosevelt*, fitted into twenty volumes.[20] He cast the president's life as a "tragedy" for the writer, whose literary achievement was swallowed almost whole by his political accomplishments. "What I want to suggest is that, apart from being a patriot and a Republican, Roosevelt bore the hallmark of a genuine man of letters and, had he devoted his life altogether to composition, he would have gained for himself a position in American literature equaled by few other men."[21]

His most enduringly popular book, *The Rough Riders* (1899), tells the story of his rugged regiment during the Spanish-American War, a tale so focused on himself that the satirist Finley Peter Dunne's comic character Mr. Dooley, in reviewing the book, quipped, "But if I was him I'd call th' book 'Alone in Cubia,'" a line that delighted even President Roosevelt.[22] Historians have admired his first published book, *The Naval War of 1812* (1882), a meticulous study in the genre of naval history—ironically, British readers so admired the book that it became a guide for the writing of *The Royal Navy, a History from the Earliest Times to the Present* (1897) by William Laird Clowes, who invited Roosevelt to write the segment on the War of 1812. Brander Matthews, Columbia professor and president of the Modern Language Association in 1910, thought the book that ranked in the first class was Roosevelt's *The Winning of the West*, a long history written devotedly in the tradition of Francis Parkman's *The Oregon Trail*. The distinctive sound of Theodore Roosevelt's political voice has influenced all sorts of writers, most especially Ernest Hemingway, whose ethos echoes *The Strenuous Life*. It is not too much to say that the western novel grew out of Theodore Roosevelt's narrative sketches of ranch life and game hunting: *Hunting Trips of a Ranchman* (1885), *Ranch Life and the Hunting-Trail* (1888), and *The Wilderness Hunter* (1893). Wesleyan University professor Richard Slotkin notes that Roosevelt, a founder of the Boone and Crockett Club, was the author of the frontier West's "myth of origin."[23] His books, together with the work of the artist Frederic Remington and Owen Wister's seminal western novel *The Virginian: A Horse-*

man of the Plains (1902), fashioned the myth of the American West in the 1880s for readers across the nation and the world. Remington's popular illustrations appeared in several of Roosevelt's own books, and Wister, who was Roosevelt's buddy from Harvard, dedicated the novel to him. Later in his writing career, Roosevelt's *African Game Trails* (1910) and *Through the Brazilian Wilderness* (1914) became models of how to tell expedition stories on a grand scale.

This book follows the arc and struggles of Roosevelt's literary career. Early in life, he emulated the calm prose of a scientific naturalist; later he sought the stern objectivity of a historian; and after taking public office, he amplified and simplified his voice, believing that what people want from politicians are platitudes and iterations. All the time, in the background of his public persona, Theodore Roosevelt felt more at home in nature, travel, and adventure writing, an inclination that garnered more readers, then and now. As we count them, he wrote forty-two books and cowrote another six books. By any measure, he was a prolific writer, one who strove to push his ideas into imaginative prose, and we recognize, even in the shadow of his political life, a distinctive "American-American" voice.

Chapter 1
"Not Unmusical Clangor"

What is needed is not the ability to see what very few
people can see, but to see what almost anybody can see,
but nobody takes the trouble to look at.
{ Theodore Roosevelt, "My Life as a Naturalist," 1918 }

In tarpaulin jackets, hip boots, and sou'westerly hats, Theodore and Elliott Roosevelt set out to hunt ducks along Long Island Sound on a blustery day in the late fall of 1880. The young men eyed the gray snow clouds overhead as they chipped through shore ice, rowed out to a twenty-one-foot jib-and-mainsail boat, and eased it into the harbor. In the far-off distance, they heard the mocking cry of the long-tailed duck, known locally as "old squaw" or "Sou-Sou Southerly" in mimic of its song. That "not unmusical clangor" served as the title of Theodore Roosevelt's first hunting story, an imaginative effort to turn experience into language and language into art.

"When, with November, the cold weather had fairly set in, then the old squaws come down from the north in full force," he begins; "great flocks of many hundreds, or even thousands can be seen in the open mid-waters of the sound, but they do not come into the harbours till some day when a heavy northeaster begins to blow." The young hunters risk the perils of the icy storm for a day of shooting. A "splendid, checker-back loon" appears in a shallow cove and dives instinctively to outsmart the hunters. The luck of the morning favors the young men, who deliver a "load of swan-shot" into its neck. The loon turns belly up in the water.

Sou-sou southerlies goad the young men into narrow channels and along rocky shoals, perilous places for their sailing craft. The boat's bottom grates against sunken rocks, and the "bare ribs of the wreck of an old coasting schooner" come into view, ominous signs of what may lie in wait. The ducks float "quietly on the surface, quacking, and pluming themselves, the white on their heads and wings showing well against the glossy black of their bodies." In deceptive calm, the hunters shoot barrel after barrel into the flock, counting with satisfaction "half a dozen floating dead and three or four cripples struggling wildly." Distracted and triumphant, the brothers begin to lose control, as the boat jolts against a sunken ledge, frees itself, and glides into open waters.

Nature menaces. "The steel gray waves showed here and there faint white tops, and our little boat keeled way over as she rushed through them, under the sharp gusts; the sun was entirely hidden and the sky had become a dull ashen gray which boded snow at no distant hour." The siren song of the prey lures the brothers down Long Island Sound, farther and farther away from the safety of home. "There must have been many hundreds in the flock, scattered about in clusters; there were so many that their continued, half-musical clangor had a most pleasing effect to the ear." The ducks ride the waves in "perfect unconcern," preening their "white-and-chestnut plumage" and uttering "the loud 'ha'-ha'-wee." The flock scares and rises into the air as the hunters "put all four barrels of no. 4 shot into them" and then four more. Amid swirling feathers, they grab a half dozen bodies; only one of the wounded escapes.

Other old squaws brace for the storm in the shelter of the shore, as the young hunters slip into icy shallows. Salt spray crystallizes on the gun barrels. Finally sensing danger, they turn "almost dead against the wind" and struggle to set the sheets as they tack toward home. "Under the rough touch of the wind the ice-covered shrouds sang like the chords of an Aeolian harp, a fitting accompaniment to the angry roar of the waves." The prose turns lyrical: "Sometimes there would be a few minutes lull and partial clearing off, and then with redoubled fury the fitful gust would strike us again, shrouding us from stem to stern in the scudding spoon drift." Out of the shroud looms a large coasting schooner headed straight at them. Startled, the hunters sing out "helm-a-lee, helm-a-lee" in warning to the captain. The schooner slides by "going wing and wing, everything reefed down tight as could be."

A mournful cry arises, and so "weird and airy was the sound that it stirred even our dulled senses, numbed and sluggish though the cold had made them, and we rose to our feet; as the storm lulled for an instant we saw but a short way off a great northern loon, riding on the tossing winter waves as easily and as lightly as if it had been a summer calm." The wail, a keening of sorts for the checker-back loon, unnerves the hunters as they struggle toward the safety of home. "He paid no heed to us, though we were near enough to see his eyes plainly, and again uttered the loud defiant call we had first heard." Nature defies.

"Sou' Sou' Southerly" is Roosevelt's most creative piece of youthful prose, as close to fiction as anything he would ever write. The original manuscript, now in the Houghton Library, reveals assured longhand strokes with few revisions, mostly for clarity. Confidence in the first draft is characteristic of the work he would do all his life as a writer. The hunting story shows him to be, as environmentalist Daniel Philippon notes, "a gifted and sensitive observer of his environment—a young man well on his way to becoming one of the late nineteenth century's most talented writers on nature."[1]

The young writer put the manuscript into a drawer and apparently never worked to publish it, as he would do later with nearly every word he committed to paper. In 1958, the American Academy of Arts and Letters displayed the manuscript in a retrospective, "Theodore Roosevelt, Man of Letters; a Centennial Exhibition of Books, Manuscripts and Related Materials," and in 1988, *Gray's Sporting Journal* finally published the hunting story, unpacked and fresh for readers in the late twentieth century.[2] The story marked the beginning of his intrepid career as a literary man. Throughout his life, Theodore Roosevelt worked to put action and thought into journals, letters, scientific field reports, nature sketches, hunting tales, national histories, military memoirs, political speeches, academic essays, book and art reviews, editorials, and exhortations of all sorts.

His literary life can be traced to his earliest days with a pencil. The young boy was severely nearsighted and, for the first thirteen years of his life, did not know it. Two strengths, crucial to good writing, grew from his myopia: he became an ardent reader with a nearly photographic memory and developed a sharp ear for sounds around him.[3] The Roosevelt children lived in a late Victorian household with wealthy parents who indulged their eccentricities. Tedie began writing letters at an early age; one to his mother Martha Bulloch Roosevelt as she visited her girlhood home in Georgia sounds strikingly like the voice we hear even in the last letters he would write before his own death in 1919.

"I have just received your letter! What an excitement," the young boy beams. "What long letters you do write. I don't see how you can write them." The outside world thrills the boy: "I jumped with delight when I found you heard the mocking-bird, get some of its feathers if you can." To his father, he flatters, "Your letter was more exciting than Mother's," as he puts in another order. "You know what supple jack's are do you not?" He wants two supple jack vines: "Ask your friend to let you cut off the tiger-cat's tail and get some long moss and have it mated [matted] together." A note to his sister Corinne bristles with young life. "I have got four mice two white-skinned, red eyed, velvety cretures very tame for I let them run all over me they trie to get down the back of my neck and under my vest and two brown-skinned, black-eyed soft as the other but wilder."[4] Tedie Roosevelt was already a writer.

Beginning in his ninth year, he crafted journals filled with percep-tions, enthusiasms, and turns of phrase that set patterns for his later es-says and books and speeches. "Three Weeks of My Life Age Nine Years" details a family holiday that turned out to be cold and rainy. The chil-dren played outside whenever possible, and when indoors, they "read, wrote, or drew."[5] Those three activities — reading, writing, and drawing — shaped his young mind. Childhood, for the Roosevelt children, was full of books; they read together, often with their father reading aloud, and they read privately for hours, Tedie sometimes indulging in a book a day. He read novels over and over again, committing favorite lines and passages to memory, a habit he would follow all his life. The children learned how to write letters to each other and to friends and were encouraged to keep track of their activities and thoughts in journals.

Tedie proved to be especially talented in sketching from nature. In "Natural history on insects. By Theodore Roosevelt," he declares: "All these insects are native of North America. Most of the insects are not in other books."[6] After detailing twenty-five species, including ants, spiders, ladybugs, and butterflies, as well as hawks and crayfish, the boy professes his scientific method in a postscript: "All these stories were gained by ob-servation." He also wrote "My expeditions and adventures," a collection of three stories about his experiences in nature, one about rowing a boat to the bottom of a waterfall, another about being chased by wild dogs, and a third about riding on horseback. Even more remarkably, he filled one journal with pictographs that he titles "Attempts at writing Indian sign language," followed by a graphic story of battle and defeat.[7] These jour-nals, each written from a different perspective, display the boy's literary tendencies. From observation, his myopic eyes record what they see; from experience, he tells tales of the natural world; and from study, he imagines the past. He was becoming a science writer, a nature writer, and a histo-rian, modes he would work all his life to perfect.

In May 1869, the Roosevelt family began a year's tour of Europe that

Tedie reported in a set of journals. The family docked in Liverpool, where they visited his mother's brothers, James and Irvine Bulloch, both Civil War heroes, albeit on the side of the Confederacy. The boy's voice, for the most part, is honest, straightforward, and unsentimental as he grows from ten to eleven years of age, recording what he sees, often in quirky glimpses of the periphery. Take, for instance, his story of a day in Chatsworth, a distance of seventy-two miles from Liverpool. He starts in the early morning on a walk with his sister Corinne: "We saw some darling little puppies just born. We drove on to Haden hall an old feudal castle of the 11th century. We saw the pewter plates to cook and eat with. The Leathern jacket in which a lord received his death wound. We saw the dining room and kitchen with its huge fire place and a bedroom with its bed in it and some tapestry."[8] The journal turns to images that attract the boy himself: "On this last was a picture of a boar hunt in which the dogs were in armour. The coat of arms was a bear and bull with shield." After the tour, he is still observing: "We drove on among wild and picturesque scenery to the New bath hotel. We chased ducks there and found a dead gosling in the river. After a while took cars to Liverpool. Saw a huge oak." The narrative moves from morning to evening, marking the events that catch his eye: puppies, pewter plates, a jacket with a death wound, a tapestry of a boar hunt, and wild scenery. The day ends with a dead gosling as it had begun with newly born puppies, but the young writer doesn't catch the irony or poignancy of birth and death. His last image of a huge oak tree is not a symbol, just a tree. The prose is unadorned but sure-footed.

As they travel to Italy, he experiments with sentiment. With one of his legs in Italy and the other in Switzerland, the countryside becomes for him "the true Italy of the poets."[9] He indulges in solitude: "I strayed from the rest and now in the wood around the villa Colata, which is on Lake Como with no sound save the waterfall and the Italian breeze on my cheek. I all alone am writing my Journal."[10] Three days later, he gushes, "Let the aniverserry of the morning of the day as one of the greatest humiliations and losses of my life. I lost my watch to day." Marking the precisions of time, crucial to the young boy's rhythms, the watch was precious to him, making its loss seem like the end of the world.

He surrenders to melancholy especially on Sundays as the family rests and he has little to do. As he sits alone by the fire, a wave of homesickness comes over him, reminding him of his favorite poet Henry Wadsworth Longfellow's "The Slave's Dream." In the poem, a slave who was once an African king dreams "in the mist and shadow of sleep" about his native land, just as the languishing Tedie Roosevelt feels himself a slave to the family vacation and pines for New York.

Longfellow wrote,

Wide through the landscape of his dreams
The lordly Niger flowed;
Beneath the palm-trees on the plain
Once more a king he strode.

Tedie's version went like this:

Again he is a king by the banks of the niger
Again he can hear the wild roar of the tiger.

He works to make his misery clear: "Again I was lying by the roaring wood fire (with the cold October wind shrieking outside) in the cheerful lighted room and I turned round half expecting to see it all again and stern reality forced itself upon me and I thought of the time that could come never, never, never."[11]

He kept count of the days and on November 12 cheered, "We have been half the time we are to stay abroad! hip! hurrah!"[12] And ten days later, as a comfort, his mother showed him a picture of Edith Carow (a childhood friend who would become, much later, his second wife), and he laments in his journal, "her face stired up in me homesickness and longings for the past which will come again never, alack never."[13] But he was not a child who suffered long. At the end of a day in December, he proclaims, "The sunset was splendid. No words can describe it. It were folly to try to describe it."[14] After reporting the events of the day, a thirty-seven-mile tour that included a good deal of brisk walking, he enthuses, "On the whole I have had as nice a time as I ever have had." Characteristically, he delights in living and shrugs off disappointments.

The family traveled luxuriously, pushed only occasionally into contact with the poor. One day stands out for what Tedie naïvely reveals about the callousness of a wealthy Gilded Age family on holiday. On a December day, riding and walking through a landscape dotted with castles, they stop to enjoy a picnic lunch and find themselves pestered by beggars. They hire one beggar to keep off the rest. "Then came some more fun," the boy confides. "Papa bought two baskets of doughey cakes. A great crowd of boys, girls and women. We tossed the cakes to them and I fed them like chickens with small pieces of cake and like chickens they ate it."[15] His father's friend wields a whip, pretending to use it on a small boy, forcing

THEODORE ROOSEVELT

them all to open their mouths as he tosses cakes into them. For what Tedie calls a "coup de grace," they throw the cakes into a pile and laugh at the "writhing heap of human beings." The family delights in the scene as they force the crowd to give "three cheers for U.S.A." The journal continues, "We drove on verry soon in the moonlight. It was beautiful." The only grumble was that their hotel has no parlor.

There are signs that Tedie was different from his family. The long year of tourist sights and lectures wore on the boy, who preferred playing with his siblings or writing in his journal; he came to dread yet another exhibition of European splendor. On January 8, 1870, for example, he thrills: "Mr. Stevens Papa Ellie and I had a great play with orange peels. We had great fun. We are at a station. . . . We are at another station. We have been passing through hilly country." When the entourage arrives finally at Caserta, Italy, visiting a villa full of statues and pictures, the boy moans, "We went through the rooms which though verry rich were dreary beyond expression."[16] What catches his eye on the way out is "a little bird frozen to death." In Rome, the children are rowdy and rebellious, and Tedie's prose blazes: "We then began to chase with gun and sword dogs. We saw 2. We charged rat a tat, rat a tat went our feet, bang, bang went the two guns, clash, clash went the swords, bow wow went the dogs and ran and we also."[17]

Most often, he makes himself the central figure in the family drama, and there is plenty of evidence beyond his journals that his parents doted on him, especially during his episodes of asthma. What he called his "asmer" showed up on the very first page of his journal when he was nine and plagued the young boy, as biographer David McCullough artfully details in *Mornings on Horseback*. His mother petted him; his father took him on rigorous rides and walks both morning and night, meant to stimulate his breathing and make him stronger than the malady. Whenever he reveled in rough play, signs of the "asmer" disappeared from his journals.

The boy wrote little when he was bored and sedentary. As the family returned to New York in May 1870, he lost track of his journal. The next family trip to New England, in August 1871, rekindled his writing. His journal "In the Adirondacks and White Mountains" describes glimpses of lush mountain slopes and sightings of bald eagles as the Roosevelts move up Lake George in a steamboat. "The scenery at this point is so wild that you would think that no man had ever set foot there," he imagines.[18] The family took a stagecoach for the ride to Lake Champlain, and the boy reports a violent exchange with a man challenging their right to the seats:

"At this moment the horses backed and he was thrown under their heels whence he was at length extracted but not before he had received serious injuries."[19] Tedie faithfully records what he sees without comment on social privilege.

In the landscapes of eastern New York and Vermont he found remnants of military history that delighted him. His eye catches sight of the ruins of Fort Ticonderoga, and he remembers tales of Ethan Allen who "gallantly took" the fort. When the family reaches Plattsburgh, the boy thrills to tales of the battle of Lake Champlain on September 11, 1814, the naval victory that ended the British invasion of the northern states. As he stands outside overlooking the bay, the locals give him a cannonball from the great battle. The history that the boy begins to absorb, as he clutches the cannonball, will emerge in his first book, *The Naval War of 1812*.

As the men and boys and their guides traveled by boat down the Saint Regis River, portaging and camping along the way, the boy records spotting wild ducks, loons, a great blue heron, and a kingfisher, along with deer, wolves, bears, and a mink and a grouse. His father packs James Fenimore Cooper's *The Last of the Mohicans*, the epic tale of Indians and the French battling the British in 1757. Tedie confesses in his journal: "Father read aloud to us from 'The Last of the Mohicans.' In the middle of the reading I fell asleep. Father read by the light of the campfire."[20] Cooper's fiction would never much appeal to the son.

As a boy, indeed all through his life, Theodore Roosevelt felt more alive when he was moving around. He delighted in writing about the next family trip abroad in "Journal of Travels to Europe, Including Egypt and the Holy Land," from October 1872 to May 1873. By that time, he literally looked out on a wider world, more colorful and precise, because—his parents having discovered his myopia—he could see it through a new pair of spectacles. They sailed into Liverpool to join his Uncle Bullochs just days before Theodore celebrated his fourteenth birthday on Sunday, October 27, 1872. On Monday, Martha Roosevelt took her children to be fitted for clothes, hats, and jewelry, but her son bought himself some dead snipes and partridges, having just purchased arsenic to prepare the skins of birds he was collecting into what the children called the Roosevelt Natural History Museum. His desire for arsenic, a full pound, raised eyebrows in Liverpool, and he had to bring a witness to vouch for his desire to practice taxidermy, not commit murder, much less suicide.[21] His birthday gifts after dinner included "one bag, two pens, two pencils, one inkstand, two penknives"—gifts for an intellectual child, given to writing and reading and skinning. During his birthday week, he shopped for scientific books; not finding what he wanted, he borrowed a copy of Audubon's works from his aunt and spent much of his days in Liverpool reading.[22]

Traveling through Germany, France, and Italy, the family reached Alexandria on November 28, where he shouts into his journal, "How I gazed on it! It was Egypt, the land of my dreams; Egypt the most ancient of all countries!"[23] His imagination unfolds: "It was a sight to awaken a thousand thoughts, and it did." Looking through his spectacles, he compares the vastness of the desert to the ocean and to the North American prairies. The expanse of human history at Pompey's Pillar, however, leaves him speechless, "On seeing this stately remain of former glory I *felt* a great deal but I *said* nothing. You can not express yourself on such an occasion."

At fourteen, Theodore witnessed dazzling Cairo street scenes during what he calls the "Procession of Mahommets Cloth (I do not know its other name)." In a signature voice, he declares: "I have never spent a more amusing and interesting hour in my life."[24] The street procession had more to offer the eye than he had ever had the opportunity to see. "All sorts of men and beasts were continually passing. Various races of men could be recognized, such as the white, black, Egyptian and Eastern white, Arab or Syrian." For the first time, he notes that a mysterious female, "a beautiful Circassian Lady, inmate of some rich mans Harem, was looking (with the vail dropped) out of a window above us . . . and appeared to have no objection to be openly admired by Father." He gazes on his father who gazes on the woman who gazes back. The boy shyly avoids the obvious question: what could be the meaning of the dropped veil?

The young writer, fresh from reading Audubon, was more comfortable detailing the natural world. "The crow is of grayish or white colour, with black wings, tail and head and of about the size of an ordinary crow. Numbers were to be seen sailing overhead, perched on the trees, or *walking* (not hopping) about the ground in search of food, unheeding and unheeded by both men and birds."[25] He learned to hunt the very birds he was watching. "In the morning Father and I went out shooting and procured two small warblers and blew a chat to pieces in the walk of a hundred yards. One of these was the first bird I had ever shot and I was proportionately delighted." He may well have been the one who blew the chat to pieces; he always admitted that he wasn't a good shot. For Christmas, his father gave him "a beautiful breechloading double barreled shot gun," and Theodore Roosevelt's life as hunter began in earnest. Over the winter months, he records no bouts of asthma and, at times, lists only his kills for the day, carefully printing the Latin names of doves, sand snipes, larks, herons, hawks, hoopoes, starlings, pigeons, owls, plovers, and pelicans. Trained in taxidermy by John G. Bell, a man who had once traveled with Audubon, Tedie Roosevelt displayed considerable skill in mounting a group of Egyptian plovers that stand to this day in the American Museum of Natural History in New York City.

The journals document the young writer's experiments with the language of science, a sign of his desire to become a field zoologist and, more specifically, an ornithologist. "I saw an Ibis too," he wrote in a typical passage on January 8, 1873:[26]

> I may as well describe the habits of the Ibis. It is in reality a *heron* and *not* an ibis, far less the sacred Ibis, which is not found in Egypt. It is very common in Egypt and very tame, being never molested by the natives, and but little by the travellers. Although a water bird is very frequently seen inland, acting the part of the crow or rook in following the plough to pick up the grubs turned up with the soil, or wandering in the fields, insect hunting on its own account. I have also seen it wading in the shallows, apparently fishing. It seems stra[n]ge that a heron should roost on treetops but such is the fact with this bird. While near Cairo, opposite the Island of Rhode (which is thickly covered with trees, and to which these birds resort) I used to watch them by the hour.

And watch by the hour he did, stealing time away from cultural tours to devote attention with eye and pen to the truth before him, dispelling myths he had learned from books. The pattern of his later writing as a field scientist was established, in rough form, in these early journals.

In letters home, Tedie hones his writing skills, repeating and refining language. On a visit to Karnak, for example, he writes first in his journal that they had visited "Harnak" by moonlight: "It seemed to take me back thousands of years, to the time of the Pharohs [*sic*] and to inspire thought which can never be spoken, a glimpse of the ineffable, of the unutterable."[27] Both "ineffable" and "unutterable" are new words in his vocabulary, and one wonders where he got them, from his father or a guide? He works the new words into his letter to Aunt Anna: "We are now on the Nile and have been on that great and mysterious river for over a month. I think I have never enjoyed myself so much as in this month."[28] Karnak is without parallel: "I never was impressed by anything so much. To wander among those great columns under the same moon that had looked down on them for thousands of years was awe-inspiring; it gave rise to thoughts of the ineffable, the unuterable; thoughts which you can not express, which can not be uttered, which can not be answered untill after The Great Sleep." Then he tells her about the new shotgun that he carries with him along the shore every day but Sunday and brags that his largest kill is a crane. And in a cheeky aside, he reports that the children along the Nile up to the age of ten are wearing "nothing."

The family continued traveling from Egypt through the Holy Land, where one site especially impressed him: "What I did awe for, was to think that on the very hill which the church covers was the place where Jesus was crucified."[29] By the time they reached the Wailing Wall, however, he had begun to question the sincerity of worshippers: "Many of the women were in earnest, but most of the men were evidently shamming."[30] The family bathed in the Dead Sea—"Of course we bathed in it"—and traveled through Syria and Lebanon and by steamer to Athens, passing through the Dardanelles to Constantinople. The Mosque of Hagia Sophia dazzled Tedie in its Byzantine splendor: "This is by far the most beautiful one I have yet seen, being composed of marble, Porphry, verdantique, and the Dome with mosaics."[31] But by the time they reached Vienna, Theodore returned to dissecting rabbits and skinning birds. "I bought black cock and used up all my arsenic on him," he fumed, admitting that the weeks in Vienna were dreary: "If I stayed here much longer I should spend all my money on books and birds '*pour passer le temps.*'" The journal stopped in Dresden as the children were left with the Minkwitz family for the summer to study German.

In his letters Theodore is amiable and witty. Having an audience clearly in mind brings his prose to life; and reading his letters today, we can see signs of the nascent politician who shifts tone to suit his purpose. The letters to his mother are aimed at her sense of responsibility for the children's well-being; thus his letter on May 19, 1873, plays on her anxiety over Corinne as a cover for his own irritations and the discomforts of his asthma. "If there is anyone to be uneasy about it is Corinne. A more doleful little mortal than she is it would be hard to imagine," he warns her, offering a solution: "I think a letter to the effect that she will only stay here a month would comfort her greatly."[32] He whines about having to learn twenty-five German prepositions all at once and that learning French is even harder. And he tattles on the Minkwitzes, who gossip in German about the Roosevelts without knowing that the boy understands what they thought they were saying behind his back. In a letter to Aunt Anna,

Tedie pokes fun at the fussiness of the Germans: "My scientific pursuits cause the family a good deal of consternation. My arsenic was confiscated and my mice thrown (with the tongs) out of the window." He attaches a mocking sketch of his plan for retribution, "I would approach a refractory female, mouse in hand, corner her, and bang the mouse very near her face." He grumbles to a friend, Mr. Godey, that it was the maid who had the "unpleasant habit of throwing my mice or bats that I bring home to skin out of the window, much to my sorrow and disgust."[33] He laments that life in Dresden is monotonous: "It reminds me of the boys [in *Oliver Twist*] who were fed on meal and mush for six days in the week, a week, and on Sundays (for a variety) on mush and meal." To his father, Theodore boasts his accomplishments. "The German is getting on very well and the French teacher says that if I knew the tenses of the verbs I would have a very good knowledge of the French language. I can read it just and understand it almost as well as English." His father had sent boxing gloves, and the son brags about a black eye: "If you offered rewards for bloody noses you would spend a fortune on me alone."

He told his father that the kids had formed the Dresden Literary American Club, but he did not tell him their motto, W.A.N.A., stood for "We Are No Asses." The club portrait shows a group of surly adolescents: Theodore, $14\frac{3}{4}$; Elliott, $13\frac{1}{2}$; cousin Maud Elliott, $12\frac{3}{4}$; Corinne, $11\frac{3}{4}$; and Maude's brother John, $14\frac{1}{2}$. In Germany to learn the language, they defiantly write in English as true American-Americans. The W.A.N.A.s practiced language by writing stories, riddles, and poems, collected into a club book that displays different literary talents. They were a family of writers, after all, who had learned as children to read, write, and draw. Tedie's "Adventures in Shopping" tells a funny story about trying to buy bullets at a shop near Saint Stephen's Church. They mistakenly ask directions to "St. Stephens Kirsche" and get "annihilated with a glance." At the shop, they stumble again with language, blurting out the letters "B-u-l-l-e-t-s" and stomping out when no one knows what they are saying. The same arrogance and wit flash in his letters home to his sister Anna. On September 21, 1873, just shy of fifteen and bored with his studies, Tedie ended a letter, "As I have no news to write I will close up with some illustrations on the Darwinian Theory."[34] He charts four evolutionary stages of man, sketching his own growth from a stork, Elliot's from a bull, and his cousin Johnny's from a monkey. There is every reason to believe that the Germans were as pleased as the W.A.N.A.s to see the Dresden adventure end.

After returning to Oyster Bay in the fall of 1873, Theodore focused his literary efforts on science writing as he collected and revised his bird descriptions into a journal titled "Ornithological Observations made in Europe, Syria and Egypt." He begins each entry with the bird's Latin name and a description. Of the vulture the novice ornithologist writes: "Thus, I found it alike in the lofty, snowcapped Lebanon Mts. and in the low, marshy Nile Delta; in the fertile plain of the Jordan and in the arid Nubian Desert. It soars at an immense height, so as frequently to become invisible and hardly ever seems to move its wings."[35] His writing is vivid, packed with visual detail. He schools himself in field biology, especially ornithology, and records what each bird looks like, how it moves, and how it sounds to the human ear. University of Pittsburgh historian Paul Russell Cutright collected Roosevelt's sketches into "The Boyhood Natural History Notebooks of Theodore Roosevelt" for a 1956 book, *Theodore Roosevelt, the Naturalist*.[36] The collection is remarkable for signs of patience, a quality not often associated with Theodore Roosevelt. He modestly jokes: "In the following paper I pretend to do nothing more than give a few observations. . . . As my opportunities for investigation have been, of necessity, limited, many errors have crept (or rather *stalked*) in."[37]

The boy would crouch quietly for hours, watching a single bird, noting every movement, behavior, even attitude, and transforming the bird's body into language. Only then would he shoot the bird, slit the stomach, empty the gut, and painstakingly measure every feathered feature —the head, the body, the feet, and the wings. In the nineteenth century, an ornithologist's expertise was measured by the collection itself, the set of skins and mountings. Many of his skins, neatly labeled and stored in the Roosevelt Natural History Museum, became the second acquisition of the American Museum of Natural History, an institution that his father helped to found (as he did the Metropolitan Museum of Art across Central Park). Theodore Roosevelt's collection continues to be housed in the museum, where today when pulling out a drawer of bird skins from the 1870s, one can spot the distinctive tags, neatly lettered by the young Roosevelt himself. Nothing in the Roosevelt acquisition astonishes more than his mounting of a lush snowy owl that he shot on Oyster Bay in 1876.

His journals reflect the literary influence of the Scottish-born poet and ornithologist Alexander Wilson (1766–1813), who wrote a nine-volume *American Ornithology*, describing the sizes and colors and habits of 268 species of birds. Wilson tended toward long narratives, often written in elaborate language. A closer prose model for Roosevelt was the French-born John James Audubon (1785–1851), whose *The Birds of America* featured 435 astonishing watercolors accompanied by descriptive prose sketches. Both writers influenced Roosevelt's choice of language, even as he worked to find a voice of his own.

Capturing the sounds of the birds proved baffling for the boy who was not musically inclined and struggled to find patterns to suggest onomatopoeia. Wilson thought the American redstart was not much of a songster, recording merely its "*weése, weése, weése.*"[38] Audubon thought the redstart's notes were lovely, resembling "the sound of *Tetee-Whee, Tetee-whee*" and "*wizz, wizz, wiz.*"[39] The young Roosevelt records the song as "zee zee" and "tseettseetseetstee, quickly and loudly repeated." He works to describe patterns that follow the sound he is actually hearing. His yellow-breasted chat mixes hard whistling notes with finer ones that "may be represented by 'keck, keck, keck, lut, lut, lut, gch gch gch gch, whew whew, sic, sic, sic." He records the chirp of the black-capped chickadee as "a low wheezy tone" in two variations, "the chick a day" and the "plaintive peé-wee." His ear is sharp enough to discriminate birdsong from one season to another. Of the white-throated sparrow, he notes "a very sweet plaintive song" in spring that differs from "its autumn notes." And he records changes in mood; the American robin, a "very noisy bird," sings "various notes to express surprise, anger, fear, etc, and uses them freely."

Roosevelt always favored the song of the wood thrush, whose "alarm note is a lengthened, chirp, much like the robin's, but lower and more liquid." The hunter in him hears the "short but rich and sweet song" of the mourning warbler but is chagrined by the difficulty of luring this motionless prey "from the nature of its haunts" so that he can get a good shot at it. The boy distinguishes the Blackburnian warbler's repertoire of a dozen different songs, "none of them particularly powerful or musical." He notes one as "weesee, weesee, weesee, tsetsetsetse" and another as "wee, see, see, tsetsetse tsetse" and adds what only a fairly sophisticated ear would hear, "a succession of slender, filing notes uttered on the ascending scale."

By 1877, Theodore was writing somewhat lyrically himself in a "not unmusical clangor." His first publication was a pamphlet, *The Summer Birds of the Adirondacks*, cataloging his youthful observations together with those of a Harvard College friend, Henry Minot. The two men described ninety-seven species, many of them unfamiliar even to the locals in the Adirondack Mountains. Theodore wrote his own entries, and in them one hears not only the music of the birds but, more so, the rhythms of his prose at age eighteen. In one of the sketches, he fills a deer-hunting story with ominous sounds: "the dull, heavy crash" of a dead tree, the "harsh hooting of an owl," and the "unholy laughter of a loon." The hermit thrush appears:

> Wearied by our unsuccess we at last turned homeward when suddenly the quiet was broken by the song of a hermit thrush; louder and clearer it sang from the depths of the grim and rugged woods, until the sweet, sad music seemed to fill the very air and to conquer for the moment the gloom of the night; then it died away and ceased as suddenly as it had come. Perhaps the song would have seemed less sweet in the daytime, but uttered as it was, with such surroundings, sounding so strange and so beautiful amid these grand but desolate wilds, I shall never forget it.[40]

The writing unfolds in cadences and turns of phrase that would continue to mark his prose. In the sweet, sad music of the hermit thrush, we can hear the airy, defiant call of the great northern loon and see the beginnings of his hunting tale, "Sou' Sou' Southerly."

At the end of his life, Theodore Roosevelt looked back on his early forays into ornithological prose in an essay, "My Life as a Naturalist." The old man dismisses the boy's accomplishments: "I made copious and valueless notes."[41] He is a hard judge: "I lacked the power to find out things that were not obvious" and, as a result, made "no particular addition to the sum of knowledge." The man who had by that time been president of the United States and, as things looked in 1918, would become president again in 1920, is somewhat indulgent with the boy who may not have been a scientist by inclination. Tedie might have taken comfort in the old man's wisdom: "What is needed is not the ability to see what very few people can see, but to see what almost anybody can see, but nobody takes the trouble to look at." In that way, the boy's curiosity and patience display genius.

In writing field notes, Theodore learned a craft that would never rise to a profession; for all his observation and writing, he would never become an ornithologist. And he had put his imaginative story, "Sou' Sou' Southerly," in a drawer. What we do know about his literary life is that he would not become a writer of science or of fiction, although both impulses are everywhere present in his first two books, one on United States maritime history, *The Naval War of 1812* (1882), and the other on life in the American West, *Hunting Trips of a Ranchman* (1885).

Chapter 2

"Chateau-en-Espagne"

> I think the Commodore may do me a good turn at the Navy
> Department, in getting me access to records for that favourite
> chateau-en-espagne of mine, the Naval History. You would be amused
> to see me writing it here. I have plenty of information now, but I
> can't get it into words; I am afraid it is too big a task for me.
>
> { Theodore Roosevelt to Anna Roosevelt, August 21, 1881 }

> The Republic is not to be despaired of, and even Albany politics,
> that Augean stable, may be still a matter for better hopes when we
> find that a rising young politician like Mr. Roosevelt has wider scope
> to his mind than wire-pulling, and has made at least one period of
> American history the object of a serious study. . . . There is seldom
> or never an attempt to do any fine writing. The style is sober and
> sometimes energetic. . . . [*The Naval War of 1812*] is an excellent one
> in every respect, and shows in so young an author the best promise
> for a good historian—fearlessness of statement, caution, endeavor to
> be impartial, and a brisk and interesting way of telling events.
>
> { *New York Times*, June 5, 1882 }[1]

At Harvard College, Theodore began studying in the conventional way with courses in language and literature, earning a 58 in Greek and a 92 in modern German. In those days, students at Harvard passed a class with a 50 and received honors in an elective class with a 70 and a required class with a 75.[2] During his sophomore year, he flourished in rhetoric with a 94, but earned a middling 69 in essay writing. His summer as a boy in Dresden had made him more than conversant in the German language, allowing him to score a 92 in a reading class and a 96 in composition. In French, he was always weak, marked by his lowest college grade, a 51, in seventeenth-century French literature. During his sophomore year, he took his only course in history, Anglo-American constitutional history, earning a respectable 89. Theodore was at Harvard primarily to study science and took comparative anatomy with William James, a course that he told his father was "interesting"; James gave him a 79. A course in botany earned him an 89, and during his junior year he did very well, a 92, in a course that combined geography, meteorology, and geology. Not surprisingly, Theodore earned his highest college grade, 97, in zoology. During his junior year, he did fairly well in English composition with 76, but struggled through a forensics class, a 60, perhaps the most dramatic surprise for a man who would become famous for a distinctive public voice. In his senior year, he earned 78 in political economy, 91 in geology, and 89 in zoology. Theodore graduated magna cum laude and Phi Beta Kappa, ranking 21st out of 158 in his class and doing well across the board, with an "honorable mention" only in his beloved natural history. He did not leave Harvard as a field biologist, the strong desire of his youthful years, and he did not show much promise as a historian. His academic record doesn't show us much about his life as a politician and even less about his life as a writer.

In the privacy of his diary and the intimacy of his letters during those years, we can hear a voice struggling to express emotion. Even at Harvard, and especially when he was away from home, Theodore's best friend was his father. Theodore senior had written his son, as he left for college, a letter of warning about the curse of alcohol on the Roosevelt family; and his son had written back on October 22, 1876, to assure him that he was not a drinker. In characteristically exultant prose, he composed the kind of letter that any parent might hold dear: "I do not think there is a fellow in College who has a family that love him as much as you all do me, and I am *sure* that there is no one who has a Father who is also his best and most intimate friend, as you are mine."[3] During his sophomore year, he knew little about his father's declining health caused by an intestinal tumor, and thus he arrived home hours after his father's death on February 9, 1878, too late to do or say anything. Bewildered, he confessed to his friend Henry Minot, "As yet it is almost impossible to realize I shall never see Father again; these last few days seem like a hideous dream. Father had always been so much with me that it seems as if part of my life had been taken away."[4]

For all of Roosevelt's public stoicism, we can see his mourning in the privacy of the diaries. He records frequent bouts of weeping, "good square" breakdowns, admitting, "if I had very much time to think I believe I should almost go crazy." He fills pages with sorrow as he struggles to map his life's course without the comfort or counsel of his father. "I should like to be a scientist," he announced to himself alone. The constant refrain in the diary throughout 1878 is the loss of his most intimate friend: "I long for him so."[5]

Theodore calculated the financial meaning of his father's death. "I am left about $8,000 [almost $180,000 in today's dollars] a year, comfortable although not rich."[6] He could look to a future of cautious spending — not his inclination — or a life of suitable work, perhaps as a writer. Theodore Roosevelt Sr., who by law had owned all the family wealth, left a third of his real and personal estate together with household items, furniture, plate, jewelry, art, books, vehicles, and horses to his wife, and divided the rest of the money into four parts, giving $60,000 in a trust fund to each child, who could draw interest and dividends as income. From the $60,000, Theodore could expect a yearly return of $8,000, a considerable sum of money for a young man who had yet to prove himself.[7] The son kept a casual count of his annual income and spending in his diaries; in 1877, he spent $1,742, and in 1878 the amount increased slightly to $2,049.45. Dress was his biggest expense at $373.45 in his sophomore year, when he spent $220.75 on his room, $305.50 on his board, and only $185.80 on his education.

The college diaries are clear about what absorbed his mind over the next two years at Harvard. In the beginning of 1879, the young ornithologist worked on the manuscript of *Birds of Oyster Bay* with Henry Minot, and hunted when possible with two outdoorsmen from Maine, William Wingate Sewall and his nephew Wilmot S. Dow, who would later work on Roosevelt's Elkhorn Ranch in the Dakotas. By the end of the school year, he crowed to his diary, "I doubt if I ever shall enjoy myself so much again."[8] What gave him such joy? He listed four accomplishments: an 87 percent overall on his grades, a horse and cart of his own for travel in Cambridge, a group of club friends, and the attention of pretty girls. What college boy could ask for more? As he returned to Harvard for his senior year, he cautioned himself, "By Jove, it sometimes seems as if I were having too happy a time to have it last."[9] Delight blossomed in his meeting Alice Lee and, by January 25, 1880, winning her hand in marriage. "The aim of my whole life shall be to make her happy," he proclaimed to his diary, calling Alice "my sweet queen!"[10] By March, as he wrote his final thesis in political economy, he laid out a plan for his life: "I shall study law next year, and must there do my best, and work hard for my own little wife."[11] The next month, he all but shouted: "no man *could* lead a more ideal life than I do."[12]

A triumphal note sounds throughout his diaries. As he moved toward graduation, the young Roosevelt proudly took his own measure: "I have certainly lived like a prince for my last two years in college."[13] Having as much money as he could spend, he again listed his joys: membership in Harvard's most exclusive Porcellian Club, frequent hunting trips, his horse and cart, a half dozen true friends, a lovely home and family, and the promise of a wife. He lifted the volume of his own praises: "*My career (both in and out of college) has been more successful than that of any man I have known*."[14]

He went hunting with his brother Elliott in the weeks before the wedding and returned to New York in glory. Yet he admitted, "My happiness is so great that it makes me almost afraid."[15] Having lost his father to an early, unexpected death, the young man, though brash and confident, knew the bitter price of love and loss. Alice and Theodore married on October 27, his twenty-second birthday, and even from his nuptial bed he tiptoed to his diary to whisper, "Our intense happiness is too sacred to be written about."[16]

Theodore scrutinized his finances. Spending had shot up over the last two years at Harvard to $5,206.59 in 1879 and $7,992.50 in 1880, a year that included buying a diamond crescent, a ruby bracelet, and a sapphire ring as wedding gifts for Alice at a cost of $2,500. "I have been spending money like water," he lamented, surprising himself.[17] His levelheaded plan to attend Columbia Law School and work at his studies every day from nine to three thirty looks much like Benjamin Franklin's earnest boyhood schedule. The diary ends on a sentimental note: "Thus ends by far the happiest year I have ever spent, for in this year I have won the fairest and purest and sweetest of women for my wife."[18] Classes began at Columbia Law School on January 4, 1881. Theodore, however, spent his afternoons at charity board meetings and his evenings with Alice at parties and sleigh rides. He joked in his diary, "working very hard at my law; have been rather loafing lately."[19] Attending an executive committee meeting of the Young Men's Republican Association, he quipped sardonically, "very hopeless."

What emerges in the diary is a literary man. "Take Alice on a long drive everyday. Am still working hard at the law school; and at one or two unsuccessful literary projects," he reported on March 24, 1881. One of those projects was "Sou' Sou' Southerly," the promising hunting tale. The other manuscript was a budding naval history that would become his first book, *The Naval War of 1812.* "Besides working pretty well at the law,

I spend most of my spare time in the Astor Library, on my 'Naval History,'" he confesses.[20] Funded by John Jacob Astor, the free public library in lower Manhattan — later part of the New York Public Library — offered the young Theodore Roosevelt a quietly elegant place to become a scholar.

On what at first glance seems to have been a diversion from his writing project, Theodore set sail with Alice on May 12 for a delayed honeymoon. "Hurrah! For a summer abroad with the darling little wife," he cheered in his diary. The European trip turned out to be a literary adventure. He confided to Anna that what was most in his mind was the book he was writing, a history of American success against the British navy on the waters of New England, the story he had first heard in Plattsburgh while camping with his father and would publish in 1882 as his first book. Reading in the Astor Library, he had begun to imagine a grandly heroic tale of naval genius and resilience. He was traveling to Europe in part to learn more.

He and Alice landed in Ireland and traveled together before crossing by ferry to Liverpool, where they stayed with his maternal uncles, James Dunwoody Bulloch and Irvine Stephens Bulloch. The siblings had grown up on the family's slaveholding cotton plantations; Martha and Irvine had been raised at their Roswell Plantation outside Atlanta. James served in the United States Navy until 1854 and then moved to Liverpool, where he purchased a Scottish merchant ship, the *Fingal*, and built a lucrative business in the cotton trade. Liverpool had become the richest city in England in the early years of the nineteenth century because it was a principal seaport for the slave trade and the subsidiary exchange of cotton, the crop that made slavery in the American South so profitable. During the Civil War, James Bulloch worked as a secret agent, negotiating cotton sales in support of the Southern cause with the financial backing of the former North Carolinian Charles Kuhn Prioleau, senior partner of the commercial house Fraser, Trenholm & Co.[21] Among his many schemes, James Bulloch organized the building of the CSS *Alabama*, the most notorious commerce raider, on which his brother Irvine served as the ship's youngest officer. Southern historians Walter E. Wilson and Gary L. McKay hail James Bulloch as a "mastermind" of the Confederate navy, and he is celebrated as a Southern war hero to this day.[22] After the Civil War, the Bulloch brothers lived in Liverpool, Uncle Jimmie bragging that he was American by birth but British by choice. As a child, Theodore had delighted in his mother's tales about her seafaring brothers. On his honeymoon in 1881, the nephew listened to his uncles' sea stories, especially details about wind-powered ships and battle tactics that he would weave into his book about the naval war of 1812.

He escorted Alice to London museums, adoring the National Gallery, especially the paintings of Rembrandt, Rubens, Reynolds, Gainsborough, and Murillo. One would think that J. M. W. Turner's seascapes would fascinate a man who was writing a book about ships and was keenly aware of natural light. Turner's impressionistic style, however, irritated Theodore, who called the painter "idiotic." From London, the young couple journeyed to Paris and Venice and Milan (where they learned that President Garfield had been shot) and then to Lucerne, Geneva, Cologne, Amsterdam, The Hague, and Brussels before returning to Paris, supposedly "devoted to the intricacies of dress buying." Theodore made a pilgrimage to Napoleon's tomb with something like reverence. "I do not think there is a more impressive sepulcher on earth," he confided to his diary. "I am not very easily awestruck, but it certainly gave me a solemn feeling to look at the plain, red stone bier which contained what had once been the mightiest conqueror the world ever saw."[23] The Napoleonic Wars, 1803 to 1815, brought the French into conflict with much of Europe on land as well as on sea, in spectacular naval battles. Even in Paris, that is to say, Theodore had his mind on the book.

"You would be amused to see me writing here," he joked to Anna from The Hague. He told her that while he was in London, he had been introduced to fellow New Yorker Commodore Charles Henry Baldwin, who had commanded the steamer *Vanderbilt* during the Civil War and sailed far and wide hunting for the CSS *Alabama*. One imagines their conversations about that hunt! He told his sister that the commodore had done him "a good turn at the Navy Department, in getting me access to records for that favourite chateau-en-espagne of mine, the Naval History." The problem wasn't finding documents, he confided, but finding his literary footing. "I have plenty of information now, but I can't get it into words," he confessed. "I am afraid it is too big a task for me. I wonder if I wo'n't find everything in life too big for my abilities."[24] Notes of anxiety appear throughout his early letters and journals as he tried to imagine where privilege and talent might take him. The Rooseveltian aspect of his youthful angst, however, was that all along he tenaciously put pen to paper.

By September, back in Liverpool with Uncle Jimmie, he was pleased to tell his mother, "As for me, I spend almost the entire time with the blessed old sea-captain, talking over naval history, and helping him to publish a work which only he possesses the materials to write, about the naval operations abroad during the last war, which were conducted and managed by him—including the cruise in the Fingal."[25] Theodore's father could not have told such stories of valor because he stayed in New York during the Civil War, perhaps because wealthy men found others to fight in their place or because his wife's family supported the Confederacy. As many biographers infer, the father's failure to fight may have triggered his son's fascination with military heroism and his desire, later in life, to fight and die in battle. In the letter, Theodore sorted out the central problem of his heritage, with half of his family on the side of the North during the Civil War ("I would have served on the Northern side") and half on the side of the South ("I do not think partisanship should ever obscure the truth"). As a writer and storyteller, Theodore was very much a Bulloch. Longing for his father, he warmed to avuncular attention. "I enjoy talking to the dear old fellow more than I can tell; he is such a modest high souled old fellow that I just love and respect him," he enthused. "And I think he enjoys having some one to talk to who really enjoys listening." The two encouraged each other, as Uncle Jimmie crafted *The Secret Service of the Confederate States in Europe; or, How the Confederate Cruisers Were Equipped* (London, 1883; New York, 1884) and Theodore *The Naval War of 1812*.

Theodore and Alice sailed to the United States on September 22, and he was back in law school classes by October 6. Alice traveled to Boston, leaving her husband to labor on the book. He confided to his diary, "Am working fairly at my law, hard at politics, and hardest of all at my book ('Naval History') which I expect to publish this winter."[26] Astonishingly, he was also entering the political arena as a candidate for the New York State Assembly from the Twenty-First District. "Have a good chance of being elected if I am not sold out," he joked in the diary. After his election, the diary went blank until December 3, when he kept his promise to himself. "Book is in the hands of the publishers—Putnam's."

Imagine the energy of a man who over the course of a year met the social expectations of his young bride, carried on the philanthropy of his dead father, attended law school at Columbia, flirted with the Republican Party and won election to the New York State Legislature, traveled for months through Europe, and all that time wrote a naval history that is still readable and, at times, enjoyable!

The Naval War of 1812 is stiff with preliminary detail, not necessarily interesting to read: as he had lamented, "I can't get it into words." Culling from official letters of commanding officers and reports of naval men in the midst of battle, Roosevelt sought truth, even as he admitted the limits of scholarship: "It is very difficult to give a full and fair account of the lake campaigns" (143). Moreover, "It is not too *easy* to reconcile the official letters of the commanders, and it is still harder to get at the truth from either the American or British writers" (145). Roosevelt's method of reporting naval equipment looks familiar to anyone who has read his boyhood journals. His early experiences with hunting birds and taking their exact measure can be seen in the meticulous way that he gauges the size and power of each frigate and brig and sloop with the precise weight of the metal shot fired and the exact number and background of the crew onboard. He drew maps of battles and sketched the shapes of vessels to make the stories clearer.

Theodore Roosevelt battled to prove himself a credible naval historian alongside James Fenimore Cooper, the American admiral George E. Emmons, and the British lawyer William James, whose books on the War of 1812 had seemed unassailable. Yet no history of the war's naval battles had faithfully delivered to the reader "matters of *fact* and not of *opinion*," Roosevelt wryly noted. "Each writer naturally so colored the affair as to have it appear favorable to his own side."[27] He promised to use naval records from both Britain and the United States, where much of the material in the Navy Department had "never been touched at all," to retell the story without bias (iv). He was pugnacious, dismissing Emmons's *Statistical History of the United States Navy* (1853) as simply "not interesting to the average reader," Cooper's *History of the Navy of the United States of America* (1856) as "without great regard for exactness," and James's *Naval Occurrences of the War of 1812* (1817) as "a piece of special pleading by a bitter and over-scrupulous partisan."

The most literary fellow in the field of naval writing was Cooper, whose *History of the Navy* served as both background and foil for Roosevelt. Much of the wit in Roosevelt's earnest history comes from his punches at Cooper, whose bent, not surprisingly, was toward fiction. Cooper, after all, had lived during the battles and had the opportunity to talk with "the actors themselves," but he was at heart a novelist. "Cooper is very inexact, and, moreover, paints every thing *couleur de rose*, paying no attention to the British side of the question, and distributing so much praise to everybody that one is at a loss to know where it really belongs" (145). However, it was the historian William James who got the full force of Roosevelt's venom, because "he is not nearly as reliable as when dealing with the ocean contests, most of this part of his work being taken up with a succession of acrid soliloquies on the moral defects of the American character" (145).

Roosevelt extolled the character of regular American sailors: "There was no better seaman in the world than American Jack; he had been bred to his work from infancy, and had been off in a fishing dory almost as soon as he could walk" (29). At the heart of the victory was the United States Navy itself, which had begun fighting the British Royal Navy with a mere half dozen frigates and six or eight sloops and brigs. Naval war in the Great Lakes and Lake Champlain, landlocked and with mild and often changeable winds, required both sides to build in place frigates, corvettes, sloops, and brigs, rigged with armaments for sea battle on a small nautical stage. The War of 1812 tested the American character, as Roosevelt understood it, and the proof of its victory was not only in the bravery of its seaman but the resilience of the navy itself as it grew during the conflict to three or four times its initial size.

A desire to rebuild the contemporary navy of the United States was at the core of Roosevelt's history. "The reason of these striking and unexpected successes," he explained, "was that our navy in 1812 was the exact reverse of what our navy is now, in 1882" (135). The young man already sounded like a savvy politician: "To bring up our navy to the condition in which it stood in 1812 it would not be *necessary* (although in reality both very wise and in the end very economical) to spend any more money than at present; only instead of using it to patch up a hundred antiquated hulks, it should be employed in building half a dozen ships on the most effective model" (136). If the naval campaigns on Lake Erie and Lake Champlain had been fought in vessels as relatively outclassed as those of 1882, he made clear, valiant American seaman would not have won a single battle. We can hear echoes of Roosevelt's talks with Uncle Jimmie Bulloch, "formerly of the United States Navy," whom he warmly thanks in his preface (vii). We can hear, too, the petulance of the future president: "It is too much to hope that our political shortsightedness will ever enable us to have a navy that is first-class in point of size" (136). Americans ought to remember that it was not the army that won the war in 1812 but rather the spirit of the navy: "As it was, our victorious sea-fights, while they did not inflict any material damage upon the colossal sea-might of England, had the most important results in the feelings they produced at home and even abroad" (136). His American reader might look upon the naval battles with "the keenest national pride" (136).

Once the fighting begins, Roosevelt's writing comes forcefully to life.

The pivotal battle of Lake Erie was one that Roosevelt dramatically described, if only so that he could debunk the myth of its place in history. Captain Oliver Hazard Perry, the most revered of American commanders of the war, came especially under Roosevelt's scrutiny. At dawn on September 10, 1813, the British under Commander Robert Heriot Barclay, who had lost his left arm in the Napoleonic Wars and was lucky to find naval duty in the backwaters of the Great Lakes, sat in wait on Lake Erie to confront Perry's fleet that had managed to cross a sandbar. "As, amid light and rather baffling winds, the American squadron approached the enemy, Perry's straggling line formed an angle of about fifteen degrees" (262). By 11:45 Barclay's ship-rigged corvette, the *Detroit*, opened fire on the brig flagship, the *Lawrence*, under Perry's command. Barclay fought well, training the guns, "though they actually had to be discharged by flashing pistols at the touchholes, so deficient was the ship's equipment" (264). The battle raged at close quarters, with the two sides about equally engaged, "the Americans being superior in weight of metal, and inferior in number of men" (265). After heavy firing on both sides, Captain Barclay quit the deck because of an injury to his right arm, and the *Detroit* itself lay shattered.

"But on board the *Lawrence* matters had gone even worse, the combined fire of her adversaries having made the grimmest carnage on her decks. Of the 103 men who were fit for duty when she began action, 83, or over four fifths, were killed or wounded," Roosevelt described the bloody scene. "The vessel was shallow, and the ward-room, used as a cockpit, to which the wounded were taken, was mostly above water, and the shot came through it continually, killing and wounding many men under the hands of the surgeon" (265). The *Lawrence* itself was mortally wounded: "Every brace and bowline was shot away, and the brig almost completely dismantled; her hull was shattered to pieces, many shots going completely through it, and the guns on the engaged side were by degrees all dismounted" (265–66). Her crew lay wounded as well: "As the crew fell one by one, the commodore called down through the skylight for one of the surgeon's assistants; and this call was repeated and obeyed till none were left; then he asked, 'Can any of the wounded pull a rope?' and three or four of them crawled up on deck to lend a feeble hand in placing the last guns" (266). Roosevelt's tone is earnest, even as the scene has the look of parody. Who can fight with a crew of wounded men crawling into battle? Captain Perry, together with his younger brother Matthew (who would later rise to the rank of commodore, the highest in the U.S. Navy), abandoned ship in a rowboat to take command of the *Niagara*, which had been positioned to the rear of the battle, and used "the fresh Brig" to tear again into Barclay's line at 2:45.

At times—such as this one—Roosevelt echoes Cooper, who had written of the *Niagara*: "In passing she poured in her broadsides, starboard and larboard, ranged ahead of the ships, luffed athwart their bows, and continued delivering a close and deadly fire" (Cooper, 192). Roosevelt, too, used the phrase "luffed athwart their bows," altering the sentence but keeping the image: "The *Niagara* luffed athwart their bows, with half pistol-shot, keeping up a terrific discharge of great guns and musketry, while on the other side the British vessels were raked by the *Caledonia* and schooners so closely that some of the grape shot, passing over the foe, rattled through Perry's spars" (267). Cooper continued the personification: "The shrieks from the *Detroit* proclaimed that the tide of battle had turned." Roosevelt chose milder prose, "Nothing further could be done, and Barclay's flag was struck at 3 P.M., after three and a quarter hours' most gallant and desperate fighting." The victory of Lake Erie, Roosevelt told his readers, was especially significant in giving "us"—and we hear the personal pronoun—command and confidence.

What to make of Perry's victory? Every schoolboy had read about Perry and the battle of Lake Erie as the crowning victory of the war, but Roosevelt was not so sure. "The simple truth is, that, where on both sides the officers and men were equally brave and skillful, the side which possessed the superiority of force, in the proportion of three to two, could not help winning" (271). Given the fact that the British threw half as much metal, it should come as no surprise that the Americans won the battle. Roosevelt actually faulted Perry for putting the vessels in an ineffective line for battle on such a day that offered little wind and calm waters, with the heavy armament of the *Niagara* to the rear, leaving the way open for the British to pummel the lighter brig in the vanguard. The *Niagara* was free to win the day because its heavy weapons could easily overwhelm the already shattered flagship *Detroit*. He honored Perry, not so much for bravery and skill during the battle, but for his foresight in building vessels and arming them in the first place. In this way, Roosevelt used Perry's reputation to advance his own argument for building a navy. "Here his energy and activity deserve all praise," he shouted, "not only for his success in collecting sailors and vessels and in building the two brigs, but above all for the manner in which he succeeded in getting them out on the lake" (274). Victory comes from preparedness.

The battle of Lake Erie set the stage for the story that Theodore Roosevelt had waited much of his young life to tell, the battle of Lake Champlain, in his mind the greatest naval battle of the war. We can see Tedie Roosevelt standing with his father in front of the hotel in Plattsburgh clutching the cannonball. Perhaps it was at that moment, as he listened to local tales about the fight, that Captain Thomas Macdonough became the true naval hero of the War of 1812.

What a sea battle it turned out to be under Roosevelt's pen! Lake Champlain, a stretch of freshwater 163 miles long but only 14 miles wide, divided by a string of islands, offered a relatively small arena for the battle in Plattsburgh Bay. The British had constructed a frigate, the *Confiance*, and had at the ready a brig, two sloops, and twelve or fourteen gunboats. The Americans had built a large brig, the *Eagle*, to accompany a heavy corvette, the *Saratoga*, along with a schooner, a small sloop, and ten gunboats or row-galleys. The guns were in place, although the converted schooner *Ticonderoga* used pistol flashes at the touchholes of the guns, as Barclay had been forced to do on Lake Erie.

Macdonough, commander of the flagship *Saratoga*, anchored first in Plattsburgh harbor to defend two thousand American troops and await the attack of the British fleet under Captain George Downie. British historians had falsely described their countrymen as underdogs in the battle, Roosevelt claimed: "None of these historians, or quasi-historians, had made the faintest effort to find out the facts for themselves, following James' figures with blind reliance" (318). The idea at the heart of William James's history was that the British had been defeated in the naval war because their vessels and crews and firepower had not been equal to the local American force. How else could a fledgling American fleet rout the great British navy? Roosevelt set out to prove the odds, ten to nine in firepower, had actually favored the British on Lake Champlain.

To become the hero of the tale, Macdonough had to be the underdog. He knew the lake well, knew that the winds typically blow from north to south, and that in the New England fall, sudden and furious gales were common on the lake. He knew it would be difficult for Downie to wait for favorable winds. "Young Macdonough (then but 28 years of age)," Roosevelt introduced his hero, "calculated all these chances very coolly and decided to await the attack at anchor in Plattsburgh Bay, with the head of his line so far to the north that it could hardly be turned; and then proceeded to make all the other preparations with the same foresight" (387). The *Saratoga* was cleverly fitted with a series of kedges, or small anchors, attached to hawsers, or thick ropes, in a spring-like system that allowed the crew to quickly flip the ship end to end in order to provide fresh guns in the battle. "The morning of September 11th opened with a light breeze from the northeast," Roosevelt began, as Downie's fleet weighed anchor at dawn and headed down the lake.

Unable to resist writing in his own *couleur de rose*, the young historian placed his hero on the deck of the *Saratoga* that morning: "As the English squadron stood bravely in, the young Macdonough, who feared his foes not at all, but his God a great deal, knelt for a moment, with his officers, on the quarter-deck; and then ensued a few minutes of perfect quiet, the men waiting with grim expectancy for the opening of the fight" (389). Sanctity gave way to levity. The first British shots fell short except for a direct hit on the hencoop of the *Saratoga*. "There was a game cock inside, and, instead of being frightened at his sudden release, he jumped up on the gun-slide, clapped his wings, and crowed lustily" (390). What could be a clearer sign? The men laughed and cheered as Macdonough returned the first fire, a direct hit that killed or wounded several men.

Roosevelt described the almost human plight of the British flagship *Confiance*: "But she was baffled by shifting winds, and was soon so cut up, having both her port bow-anchors shot away, and suffering much loss, that she was obliged to port her helm and come to while still nearly a quarter of a mile distant from the *Saratoga*" (390). The *Saratoga* likewise suffered: "Her hull shivered all over with the shock [of the enemy broadside], and when the crash subsided nearly half of her people were seen stretched on deck, for many had been knocked down who were not seriously hurt."

Foremost among the heroes were the captains on both sides. "Macdonough himself worked like a common sailor, in pointing and handling a favorite gun," Roosevelt wrote admiringly. "While bending over to sight it a round shot cut in two the spanker boom, which fell on his head and struck him senseless for two or three minutes; he then leaped to his feet and continued as before, when a shot took off the head of the captain of the gun and drove it in his face with such a force as to knock him to the other side of the deck" (392–93). The young Macdonough was clearly having trouble keeping on his feet, but Captain Downie, the would-be hero on the British side, had it even worse. "Very shortly after the beginning of the action her gallant captain was slain," Roosevelt explained. "He was standing behind one of the long guns when a shot from the Saratoga struck it and threw it completely off the carriage against his right groin, killing him almost instantly" (393). It is the "almost" that stays with the reader. "His skin was not broken; a black mark, about the size of a small plate, was the only visible injury." Roosevelt added poignantly, "His watch was found flattened, with its hands pointing to the very second at which he received the fatal blow."

Macdonough continued to prove his ingenuity by bringing his spring-action kedges into play. After the bolt on his single carronade broke, the gun fell into the hatch. "The battle would have been lost had not Macdonough's foresight provided the means of retrieving it" (395). Maneuvering the kedges, he swiveled the ship around so that the guns on its port side could fire on the *Confiance*, leaving the men free to pass the fallen gun starboard for more volleys. The masts of the *Confiance* stood, "splintered till they looked like bundles of matches; her sails had been torn to rags, and she was forced to strike," two hours after she first fired. The British second-in-command, Captain Pring, sent to know the fate of Downie, and then "the plucky little brig hauled down her colors." Macdonough, ever a gentleman, returned the British swords after the surrender, and Pring himself noted "the humane treatment the wounded have received. . . . His generous and polite attention to myself, the officers, and men, will ever after be gratefully remembered" (398). The battle scene ended in heroic gallantry, making us all wonder what such well-mannered young men were fighting about in the first place.

Roosevelt insisted, "Macdonough in this battle won a higher fame than any other commander of the war, British or American" (398). He had defeated a superior foe and thus ended British control of the inland waters. The young historian prided himself on his objectivity as a scholar. "It is to be regretted that most of the histories written on the subject, on either side of the Atlantic, should be of the 'hurrah' order of literature, with no attempt whatever to get at the truth, but merely to explain away the defeats or immensely exaggerate the victories suffered or gained by their own side" (371). He would write full-throatedly in the "hurrah" order of literature as he retold the story of his own war experience in *The Rough Riders*. But that would come later.

On May 27, 1882, the *Army and Navy Journal* praised *The Naval War of 1812*. The military reviewer thought the young writer had learned his craft: "Its easy command of materials enables the historical narrative and the comments to be interwoven without the slightest sense of dry statistics on the one hand or of superficiality on the other. The spirit of simple seeking for the truth, in which the author approaches each phase of the subject is admirable; and from the first he secures the reader's confidence." What especially caught his eye was the underlying argument that "from point to point as presented by Mr. Roosevelt in his recent book, we cannot fail to be stuck with its very direct instructions and warnings to the American Navy of to-day." The United States needed a navy in 1882 that was the equal of the navy in 1812.

The reviewer in the *New York Evening Post* agreed that Theodore Roosevelt wrote well enough for a man not interested in literary style, in and of itself. "The descriptions of engagements are clear, sober, and in good taste, and from their matter often thrilling. The effect is never injured by fine writing, and there is no attempt at the personal element appropriate to participants or to the writers of fiction." "Fine writing" came from the pens of novelists. The reviewer preferred Cooper's fiction to anything a historian might write because the battles of the war "will live longer in his novels than in his more serious narrative." But for the literal truth, should you want it, Roosevelt was the one to read.

The *New York Times* poked fun at the moral imagination of politicians in the New York State Legislature, noting a clear exception. "The Republic is not to be despaired of, and even Albany politics, that Augean stable, may be still a matter for better hopes when we find that a rising young politician like Mr. Roosevelt has wider scope to his mind than wire-pulling, and has made at least one period of American history the object of a serious study." On the quality of his writing, however, the reviewer was stern: "There is seldom or never an attempt to do any fine writing. The style is sober and sometimes energetic." The battle passages that "rise into anything like eloquence" seemed to the reviewer to have been cribbed from better writers, and yet he ends in praise of the novice: "The volume is an excellent one in every respect, and shows in so young an author the best promise for a good historian — fearlessness of statement, caution, endeavor to be impartial, and a brisk and interesting way of telling events."[28] The author, that is to say, showed the same promise as the American seamen he admired. Even as he winced, the young Roosevelt knew that his work as a literary man had begun in earnest.

British readers and historians admired his work on *The Naval War of 1812*, so much so that when William Laird Clowes wrote and edited *The Royal Navy, a History from the Earliest Times to the Present* (1897), he invited Theodore Roosevelt, who was by then New York police commissioner, together with Captain Alfred Thayer Mahan, president of the U.S. Naval War College, to write chapters on the War of 1812. Imagine

British history being written by Americans! Ever the competitor, Roosevelt wrote Clowes from Oyster Bay on December 25, 1898 — on Christmas Day! — asking when the fourth volume would be published and if it would contain his chapter. "The reason for this anxiety, as you know, is that I cannot help hoping I can get my account of the War of 1812 out ahead of Mahan's, for, of course, whatever he writes will utterly cast into the shade what I write." The letter is a famous one because of its closing line: "I suppose you saw that I was elected Governor of New York, but I think I am proudest of having been Colonel of the Rough Riders." The chapter wasn't published until 1902, and as president of the United States, Roosevelt wrote again to Clowes on February 27, sounding calmer and presidential: "It seems to me that it contains good missionary matter for both our nations."

The World Review, an Illustrated Weekly Magazine, published in Chicago, carried a consideration of Roosevelt's contribution to Clowes's history, "President Roosevelt as a Naval Historian."[29] The literary editor and poet Horace Spencer Fiske probably wrote the review: "Mr. Roosevelt has a special familiarity with this period, as the first book he ever wrote was a history of this naval conflict. He was only twenty-four at the time of writing it, and naturally his point of view was purely American." Fiske vouched for the president, who had arrived in manhood with an unprejudiced mind, one that would not offend "thoughtful and fair-minded Englishmen." He quoted Clowes: "The editor of the volume desires to make clear to his countrymen of England that although the name of the President of the United States is affixed to the chapter, the opinions expressed in it are those rather of a naval administrator, who, be it remembered, when little more than a boy, wrote what was the best American account of the war, which he now describes again, more briefly, it is true, yet by the light of fuller knowledge." Fiske praised Roosevelt for vigor and honesty of style. The focus of the review was on President Roosevelt's chief point, "the folly of a nation's reliance for security upon anything but its own full preparedness to repel attack." What emerges from his writing as a historian is the clear voice of a politician moving language into action.

Chapter 3

"Plenty of Work to Do Writing"

My work this winter has been very harassing, and I feel
both tired and restless; for the next few months I shall probably
be in Dakota, and I think I shall spend the next two or three years
in making shooting trips, either in the far West or in the Northern
Woods—and there will be plenty of work to do writing.
{ Theodore Roosevelt to Newton Dexter North, April 30, 1884 }[1]

*I*n the winter of 1883, amid the minutiae of politics in Albany, Theodore Roosevelt sang the praises of family life: "Back again in my own lovely little home, with the sweetest and prettiest of all little wives—my own sunny darling."[2] He played his usual exultant notes in the privacy of his diary: "I can imagine nothing more happy in life than an evening spent in the cozy little sitting room, before a bright fire of soft coal, my books all around me, and playing backgammon with my own dainty mistress." We note the books all around him, always within reach. The next month, he echoed his thoughts about family life in a letter to his mother, whom he called Darling Motherling: "There is nothing to me that compares with a home evening passed with those I love."[3] The diary ended abruptly for the year on January 10 and, oddly, picked up again on August 16, 1884, as musings on his second book, *Hunting Trips of a Ranchman: Sketches of Sport on the Northern Cattle Plains*, a tale of an eastern dude who "honestly imbibed something of the spirit of that wild Western life."[4] The diary simply records: "Have been spending a couple of weeks on my ranch on the Little Missouri. I now intend starting out for a ten months trip overland to the Bighorn Mountains."[5]

What happened during the missing year and more? As Theodore indulged in the pleasures of his family and learned the lessons of the political arena in Albany, his asthma troubled him, so much so that he traveled in July of 1883 with Alice to Richfield Springs, where the sulfuric waters promised full health. Sulfur springs, popular throughout the nineteenth century, offered any number of palliatives, from bathing in emollients for dermatitis to drinking purgatives for colitis. Close to Cooperstown in distance and Saratoga Springs in spirit, Richfield attracted wealthy patrons, including the Chicago tycoon Cyrus McCormick, who had just built a "cottage" designed by the New York architects McKim, Mead, and White with a garden by Frederick Law Olmsted. Sulfur springs offered the rich more than medicinal panaceas by providing an escape from the congestion and contagion of cities. Perched in the mountains, Richfield also provided fresh air for Roosevelt's lungs; the trip itself was bracing.[6] On the way up Overlook Mountain in a buggy, Theodore actually walked the four-mile trail because, ironically, his horse Lightfoot was "uncommon bad with the heaves."

Alice refused to eat what she considered "aboriginal" food, forcing Theodore to toast crackers for her "in the greasy kitchens of the grimy inns" along the way. His high-spirited letter to Corinne, whom he called "Wee Pussie," detailed the curative powers of the trip itself.[7] "But, on the other hand, the scenery was superb; I have never seen grander views than among the Catskills, or a more lovely country than that we went through afterwards." Rigorous walking in the out of doors drew mountain air into his lungs. All was well by the time they reached Cooperstown; Lightfoot "throve wonderfully," and Alice "after having eaten looked like a little pink boa constrictor." What he didn't say was that Alice ate crackers and looked like a pink boa constrictor because she was in her first months of pregnancy, fussing about food and showing a bump in her belly.

Roosevelt loathed the cures offered to them once they arrived in Richfield Springs. He described the medical man as a "heavy jowled idiot" whose ministrations caused a rapid relapse of his asthma. "I do'n't so much mind drinking the stuff," he quipped to his sister as he sipped the waters; "you can get an idea of the taste by steeping a box of sulphur matches in dish water and drinking the delectable compound tepid from an old kerosene oil can." The hot baths put him "in an ace of fainting." He awoke the next morning with an aching head and a feeling of lassitude, "bored out of my life by having nothing whatever to do." One thinks of Charlotte Perkins Gilman, whose short story "The Yellow Wallpaper" depicted a wealthy woman in the hands of "rest cure" quacks. For Theodore, the worst thing about the cure was his surroundings. Edith Wharton's satirical portraits of spas for rich New Yorkers come to mind, and here her compatriot sported as droll a pen, complaining of "being placed in that quintessence of abomination, a large summer hotel at a watering place for underbred and overdressed girls, fat old female scandal mongers, and a select collection of assorted cripples and consumptives." Roosevelt's humor was at its most irreverent when he joked with the people he loved best. He wrote his mother to say, "This place is monotonous enough to give an angel the blues."[8]

By September 1883, Theodore was ready for a manly remedy, a hunting trip in the Dakotas, considered to be curative for men suffering from the anxieties of American leisure-class living. Roosevelt's family, stunningly rich from four generations of industrious Dutch businessmen, was plagued by a variety of mental ills. Elliott, a manic-depressive who suffered from seizures (he would become addicted to alcohol and die in delirium tremens at the age of thirty-four), had gone to India, hunting tigers and elephants, and then to the Himalayas for the restorative power of life in the open. Silas Weir Mitchell famously advocated what he called the "rest cure" for wealthy women—including Gilman and Wharton and Jane Addams—but prescribed the "West cure" as the complementary treatment for men diagnosed with a variety of maladies—neurasthenia, depression, anxiety, asthma—stemming from the pressures, such as they were, of an easy life. Mitchell had begun his medical career during the Civil War, working with phantom-limb pain.[9]

After the war, in 1871, he published a study on phantom social afflictions, *Wear and Tear; or, Hints for the Overworked*, arguing that nature is curative, particularly for men. A friend and patron of Walt Whitman, Mitchell prescribed "mountain air" for the poet in 1878, a western trip recorded in Whitman's *Specimen Days*. Nature, Whitman proclaims, restored his health. "DEMOCRACY most of all affiliates with the open air, is sunny and hardy and sane only with Nature—just as much as Art is. Something is required to temper both—to check them, restrain them from excess, morbidity." American democracy, he testifies, "must either be fibred, vitalized, by regular contact with out-door light and air and growths, farm-scenes, animals, fields, trees, birds, sun-warmth and free skies, or it will certainly dwindle and pale."[10] For another friend, the painter Thomas Eakins, Mitchell advocated cowboy life in the Dakotas, illustrated luminously in Eakins's paintings, especially "Cowboys in the Bad Lands" (1888).

Theodore Roosevelt's friend Owen "Dan" Wister also took Mitchell's advice and wrote *The Virginian: A Horseman of the Plains* (1902), a seminal novel about a man's life in the American West, set in Medicine Bow, Wyoming.[11] Artists, that is to say, used the cure to think and paint and write, just as Roosevelt would do.

In a letter to Anna on September 3, 1883, Theodore announced: "Today I leave for a hunting trip in Dacotah."[12] Even as he traveled west, he kept his eye on Albany, where he was vying for Speaker of the state legislature from the minority party. In a letter to Jonas Van Duzer, a colleague who would become a confidant, he wrote what was perhaps his first autobiographical narrative, all in one sentence: "I should state that, after having passed through Harvard College, I studied for the bar; but going into politics shortly after leaving college, and finding the work in Albany, if conscientiously done, very harassing, I was forced to take up some out-of-doors occupation for the summer, and now have a cattle ranch in Dakotah."[13] He asked for Van Duzer's support of his platform based on honesty and common sense, particularly in the selection of committee members on the basis of integrity and intelligence, not patronage. "I am a Republican, pure and simple," he declared, knowing the corruption at the heart of both political parties in Albany.

"I feel now as though I had the reins in my hand," the young legislator assured his wife on January 22, 1884. Nothing could have been farther from the truth. Theodore's letters, jotted quickly from Albany to Alice, who was in New York City awaiting labor, make clear the irony of his metaphor. Their daughter was born on February 12, a birth that revealed Alice's dire case of Bright's disease. As he rushed home late the next evening, Elliott met him at the door with the news that both his wife and mother lay dying. Theodore held his mother as she died of typhoid fever in the early morning hours and then his wife later that Valentine's Day afternoon.

His 1884 diary began on February 14 with an X: "The light has gone out of my life." Two days later, he offered in this most private of places a simple tribute: "We spent three years of happiness greater and more unalloyed than I have ever known fall to the lot of others."[14] Unalloyed happiness left him utterly bereft: "For joy or for sorrow my life has now been lived out." He wrote to his colleague Andrew Dickson White, thanking him for his condolences: "There is now nothing left for me except to try to so live as not to dishonor the memory of those I loved who have gone before me."[15] Another letter to Carl Schurz on February 21 was even more revealing: "You can see I have taken up my work again; indeed I think I should go mad if I were not employed," and, echoing his diary, "though I have not lived long, yet the keenness of joy and the bitterness of sorrow are now behind me." He could say that only because he was young.

Theodore turned to his pen for solace, writing the preface to a collection of remembrances that included the full text of the funeral, together with a resolution marking the two deaths by the New York State Legislature and newspaper reports and obituaries, all published at his expense by G. P. Putnam's Sons in an elegant volume meant for the family.[16] The young man crafted language to immortalize Alice. Lying even to himself, he wrote that the birth of the baby went perfectly well and Alice had slipped into a coma, not knowing she was dying, "thinking only that she was falling into a sleep." He wrote sentimentally: "Fair, pure, and joyous as a maiden; loving, tender, and happy as a young wife; when she had just become a mother, when her life seemed to be just begun, and when the years seemed so bright before her—then, by a strange and terrible fate, death came to her. And when my heart's dearest died, the light went from my life forever." The image stunningly before him was darkness.

At the double service, Reverend John Hall, pastor of the Fifth Avenue Presbyterian Church in New York City, addressed friends and family, Theodore sitting between his brother Elliott and his father-in-law George L. Lee. Of Martha Bulloch Roosevelt, Hall's message was tranquil and clear; her husband had been "taken from her" seven years earlier; her children were grown; she had no burdens; her work was finished. The line that stayed in Theodore's mind was: "He [her husband] was more than half her life, and the hope of the reunion was a precious and present and blessed hope to her." Theodore understood that Alice, too, lay waiting for him. Hall warned the congregation and especially the young widower about "our earthly tastes and our groveling passions" and prayed in language that Theodore understood well: "Thou wilt enable him to address himself afresh to the duties that thou givest him to do, manifesting his true submission of soul to thee by the zeal, fervor, and activity with which he tries to serve thee while his life is continued on the earth." Duty, zeal, and fervor were words of comfort to the young man affronting his destiny.

Theodore returned to Albany, leaving baby Alice Lee with his sister Anna, an act that has always puzzled biographers, who find it hard to imagine that a father would abandon a baby so linked to his wife and mother. In the spring, he sketched another outline of his life for a newspaper correspondent there. "I was born in New York, Oct. 27th 1858; my father of old dutch knickerbocker stock; my mother was a Georgian, descended from the revolutionary Governor Bulloch," he began by placing himself in the world. "I graduated at Harvard in 1880; in college did fairly in my studies, taking honors in Natural History and Political Economy; and was very fond of sparring, being champion light weight at one time," he added, giving himself more credit than he had earned. And then he turned to his writing, defining himself first as an author: "Have published sundry papers on ornithology, either on my trips to the north woods, or around my summer home on the wooded, broken shore of northern Long Island. I published also a 'History of the Naval War of 1812 with an account of the Battle of New Orleans,' which is now a text book in several colleges, and has gone through three editions." He marked his life by deaths and a birth: "My father died in 1878; my wife and mother died in February 1884. I have a little daughter living."[17] And then, before listing his political work, Theodore Roosevelt limned his life as a hunter: "I am very fond of both horse and rifle, and spend my summers either on the great plains after buffalo and antelope or in the northern woods, after deer and caribou."

He wrote to Simon Newton Dexter North, the editor of the *Utica Morning Herald*, assessing his future as a politician, confiding that the political arena seemed "ephemeral" and hostile to a man who lived by ideals. With the deaths of his wife and mother most in his mind, he philosophized: "Although not a very old man, I have yet lived a great deal in my life, and I have known sorrow too bitter and joy too keen to allow me to become either cast down or elated for more than a brief period over any success or defeat."[18] His sketch is a good one to keep in mind; he would live his life between those impulses, by turns cast down and elated. Roosevelt acknowledged that he was "tired and restless" and in need of a private life as a hunter and a writer. "I think I shall spend the next two or three years in making shooting trips, either in the far West or in the Northern Woods — and there will be plenty of work to do writing."

Uppermost in his mind was "plenty of work to do writing." Life in the saddle spurred his literary imagination. He published *Hunting Trips of a Ranchman* in 1885, followed by *Ranch Life and the Hunting-Trail* in 1888, and later *Wilderness Hunter* in 1893, and *Outdoor Pastimes of an American Hunter* while president in 1905; near the end of his life, he collected bits and pieces into *A Book-Lover's Holidays in the Open* (1916). He cofounded the Boone and Crockett Club with naturalist George Bird Grinnell in 1887, and together they wrote *American Big-Game Hunting* in 1893, *Hunting in Many Lands* in 1895, and *Trail and Camp-Fire* in 1897. The writing style of his hunting stories grew directly from his boyhood journals on birding and from his literary experiment, "Sou' Sou' Southerly."

By June 17, he wrote to Anna about the joys of solitary life. He was having a "glorious time" and felt "well hardened" by physical toil. "I have just come from spending *thirteen* hours in the saddle," he enthused.

Ranching was not yet financially viable but seemed to him—never good with money—a sound investment over time. Sylvane Ferris and Arthur Merrifield partnered with him on his first venture, the Chimney Butte or Maltese Cross Ranch, and worked with him to build a second Elkhorn Ranch along the Little Missouri River. Roosevelt had lost 25 head of cattle over the winter of 1883–84 but had 155 calves and planned to hire his friends, the Maine outdoorsmen William Sewall and Wilmot Dow, who would bring their families with them, to help him run the new Elkhorn Ranch. Being in the saddle and shooting antelope had done the trick. His diary recorded the blood sport: "I leaped off as [the antelopes] passed within twenty five yards, and gave them both barrels, killing a fine buck shot through both shoulders."[19] Shooting another antelope three days later, he called it "the best shot I ever made with this rifle" and boasted to Anna, "I have never been in better health than on this trip."[20] The West cure was working.

In the background, Roosevelt kept a hand in the political world, working with Henry Cabot Lodge to resist the nomination of Blaine for president in 1884 and displaying considerable skill and energy in the battle for an independent coalition. On August 24, 1884, he wrote to Lodge from the hunting trail: "You must pardon the paper and general appearance of this letter, as I am writing out in camp, a hundred miles or so from any house."[21] He joked about the reliability of his pony express rider, "a cowboy or a horse thief," under guard and sleeping between him and his foreman. Roosevelt took issue with an *Atlantic Monthly* review of Lodge's *Studies in History*, lauding especially the sections on the Puritans: "Puritanism left if anything a more lasting impress upon America than upon England."

Hundreds of miles into the wilderness, Roosevelt could not keep away from the intellectual and political life that would draw him back to the East. "But unless I was bear hunting all the time I am afraid I should soon get as restless with this life as with the life at home," he admitted to Anna.[22] Restlessness was the very core of his being. He returned to New York in the fall and traveled west again in November in order to kill a mountain sheep and thereby complete a set of western game for the book he was working on in New York.[23]

Roosevelt was writing from diary notes, jotted at the scene, of actual kills and specific places and random embellishments. Edmund Morris makes a prescient point about a writer's life: "Roosevelt had learned, that January of 1885, the old truism that writers write best when removed from the scene they are describing."²⁴ Theodore reported to Cabot Lodge on March 8, 1885, "I have just sent my last roll of manuscript to the printer," and then he offered a tepid review of his own second book: "The pictures will be excellent—as for the reading matter, I am a little doubtful."²⁵

The book he crafted, narrative sketches by turns lyrical and brutal, blending and blurring literary genres, appeals to a modern reader. If one were to choose a single book of Roosevelt's to read, *Hunting Trips of a Ranchman* would be a good choice for its freshness and candor. The story invites us into Roosevelt's home in the Dakotas: "My home ranch house stands on the river brink. From the low, long veranda, shaded by leafy cottonwoods, one looks across sand-bars and shallows to a strip of meadowland, behind which rises a line of sheer cliffs and grassy plateaus." The veranda offers a cool breeze and a rocking chair as the writer slips his splendidly illustrated and lushly printed book into his reader's hand alongside a pile of recent books on hunting in the western United States that includes Theodore S. Van Dyke's *Still Hunter* (1882), Richard Irving Dodge's *Plains of the Great West and Their Inhabitants* (1877), John Dean Caton's *The Antelope and Deer of America* (1877), and Eliot Coues's *Birds of the Northwest* (1874).²⁶ He carefully folds himself into an American literary community of writers of all sections of the country: Washington Irving, Nathaniel Hawthorne, James Fenimore Cooper, and James Russell Lowell from the East; George Washington Cable and Joel Chandler Harris from the South; and Francis Parkman (though a Boston Brahmin) from the West. And he stretches still further to recommend "for lighter reading there are dreamy Ik Marvel, [and John] Burroughs' breezy pages" (17). Ik Marvel was the pen name of Donald Grant Mitchell, whose popular sentimental novel *Reveries of a Bachelor; or, a Book of the Heart* (1850) may have caught Roosevelt's mood.

Looking across the landscape, in a moment of synesthesia, Roosevelt hears the rhythms of Edgar Allan Poe: "And when one is in the Bad Lands he feels as if they somehow *look* just exactly as Poe's tales and poems *sound*" (17). The Badlands are called "bad" because of the dramatic distresses in contour. "This broken country extends back from the river for many miles, and has been called always, by Indians, French voyageurs, and American trappers alike, the 'Bad Lands,' partly from its dreary and forbidding aspect and partly from the difficulty experienced in traveling through it" (14). The shapes are fantastical and the colors bizarre. "When a coal vein gets on fire it makes what is called a burning mine, and the clay above it is turned into brick; so that where water wears away the side of a hill sharp streaks of black and red are seen across it, mingled with the grays, purples, and browns." And then he relents, telling his reader that even in such savage desolation, the land provides nourishing grasses and shelter from storms.

The music of the natural world consoles the writer. The meadowlark looks at first like its eastern cousin, "which utters nothing but a hard, disagreeable chatter," but, like the writer himself, finds its true voice in the Dakotas: "The plains air seems to give it a voice, and it will perch on the top of a bush or tree and sing for hours in rich, bubbling tones" (18). Certainly, that is what Roosevelt is doing. The prince of the plains birds is the Missouri skylark: "The skylark sings on the wing, soaring overhead and mounting in spiral curves until it can hardly be seen, while its bright, tender strains never cease for a moment." In the book's most lyrical language, Roosevelt records the music of a flock of snow buntings: "One bleak March day, when the snow covered the ground and the shaggy ponies crowded about the empty corral, a flock of snow-buntings came familiarly round the cow-shed, clamoring over the ridge-pole and roof. Every few moments one of them would mount into the air, hovering about with quivering wings and warbling a loud, merry song with some very sweet notes" (19).

The book, however rich the notes, is about loss. "They were a most welcome little group of guests, and we were sorry when, after loitering around a day or two, they disappeared toward their breeding haunts." As the weather turns colder, the coyotes wail uncannily and the larger wolves join in "a kind of deep, dismal howling," a keening that signals losses to come in the book (19). *Hunting Trips of a Ranchman* narrates the shooting of one stunning bird and mammal after another, arranged by prey from small to large, from passive to fierce, from easy to difficult, including a complete set of the seven kinds of plains game: whitetail deer, blacktail deer, antelope, bighorn rams or mountain sheep, buffalo, elk, and finally bear. Even in triumph as a hunter, Roosevelt sees the specter of loss: "For we ourselves, and the life that we lead, will shortly pass away from the plains as completely as the red and white hunters who have vanished" (25).

His Elkhorn Ranch offered him no more safety than his New York brownstone: "The free, open-air life of the ranchman, that pleasantest and healthiest life in America, is from its very nature ephemeral." "Ephemeral" was a word much on his mind in 1884; it was the word he used to describe the political arena in Albany and the only word to describe what

THEODORE ROOSEVELT

had become of his family life. He pressed the metaphor in the book's most eloquent passage: "The broad and boundless prairies have already been bounded and will soon be made narrow. It is scarcely a figure of speech to say that the tide of white settlement during the last few years has risen over the West like a flood; and the cattlemen are but a spray from the crest of the wave, thrown far in advance, but soon to be overtaken" (26).

Philosophically, he knew that life itself was ephemeral and that we are but spray on the crest of a wave. And unwittingly, he described the literal fate that would strike his ranch in the blizzard to come in 1886–87: "A winter of unusual severity will work sad havoc among the young cattle, especially the heifers; sometimes a disease like the Texas cattle fever will take off a whole herd; and many animals stray and are not recovered."

Losses in the West had already devastated the land and the culture. "There are now no Indians left in my immediate neighborhood," he reported, although he was not altogether sorry about that loss (23). "During the past century a good deal of sentimental nonsense has been talked about our taking the Indians' land," he wrote in a passage that makes absolutely clear attitudes that he would have his whole life (23). "Now, I do not mean to say for a moment that gross wrong has not been done the Indians, both by Government and individuals, again and again," he conceded, yet Native Americans seemed to him "treacherous, revengeful and fiendishly cruel savages." Roosevelt adhered to notions of cultural as well as biological evolution, so that for him and other social Darwinists, looking into the face of a Native American was like looking into the face of primitive man. Indians were remnants of the human past, and he would always see native peoples that way in the western United States and, later, in Africa and South America.

As for the idea of land ownership, Roosevelt hewed to European notions of property. "But as regards taking the land, at least from the Western Indians, the simple truth is that the latter never had any real ownership in it at all," he could argue with a clear conscience (24). As for fair play, he offered a simple solution. Let Indians compete alongside white settlers, every man being given 160 acres, and if an Indian should decline the offer, "let him, like these whites, who will not work, perish from the face of the earth which he cumbers." The doctrine, to his mind, was both just and rational, even as the encroachment of settlers, who fenced land in the name of business, would put an end to the West that he revered. "The cattlemen at least keep herds and build houses on the land; yet I would not for a moment debar settlers," he continued, "though their coming in means in the end the destruction of us and our industry" (24). His world was indeed ephemeral.

We hear in his voice a paean to that dying world. He lauded the old hunters of a bygone age, who headed into the American West to live a "solitary, lonely life" and wage "constant and ferocious war" against the tribes on the plains. "They rarely had regular wives or white children, and there are none to take their places, now that the greater part of them have gone" (37). The businessmen who followed on the Pacific Northern Railroad, no longer needing to face the dangers of the uncivilized West, had grown shiftless. The true heroes, for Roosevelt, were the already extinct white hunters, who were "skillful shots, and were cool, daring, and resolute to the verge of recklessness," embodying the strenuous life that would become the touchstone of his political prose. That striving to be resolute, even to the verge of recklessness, lay at the heart of the myth Roosevelt was creating about his own life.

The cowboy offered him a modern version of that manly heroism. In his diary, Roosevelt sketched the figure we all know from the popular culture that would follow in the twentieth century: "Cowboys are a jolly set: picturesque, with broad hats, loosely knotted neckerchiefs, flannel shirts, leather chaparajos."[27] In the book, he wrote: "The cowboy's dress is both picturesque and serviceable, and, like many of the terms of his pursuit, is partly of Hispano-Mexican origin. It consists of a broad felt hat, a flannel shirt, with a bright silk handkerchief loosely knotted round the neck, trousers tucked into high-heeled boots, and a pair of leather 'chaps' (chaparajos) or heavy riding overalls. Great spurs and a large-calibre revolver complete the costume" (12). The full portrait typifies Roosevelt's way of revising manuscripts with embellishments that are more specific, colorful, and detailed; rarely did he remove a word, much less a phrase, from a manuscript once he had written it firmly on paper. The mixed-race nature of the western cowboy, "Hispano-Mexican," is remarkable in that he would later rail against such hyphenations, gibing that he was American-American.

Roosevelt's prose illustrates the disruption of the western stage that he sets. Crowded into the middle of a paragraph, breaking into the scene, rides the true hero of the late nineteenth century. "In place of these heroes of a bygone age, the men who were clad in buckskin and who carried long rifles," the sentence begins, "stands, or rather rides, the bronzed and sinewy cowboy, as picturesque and self-reliant, as dashing and resolute as the saturnine Indian fighters whose place he has taken." Roosevelt continues, "and, alas that it should be written! he in his turn must at no distant time share the fate of the men he has displaced" (37). The cowboy will perish, in time, just as the old hunter had perished. The writer intrudes into the sentence, complete with an errant exclamation mark, taking center stage. Wielding a pen and a gun, Roosevelt strides onto a stage of his own making as the hero of the new West.

"I myself am not, and never will be, more than an ordinary shot," Roosevelt surprisingly confesses, "for my eyes are bad and my hand not oversteady" (42). That is an odd admission for a marksman who claims the center of the stage. With all his flaws, he boasts having killed "every kind of game to be found on the plains," because he is persevering and watchful and has good judgment and "a little dash and energy." He invites the reader, perhaps a novice hunter—perchance a bad shot too—to follow. Always keen on costume, he meticulously dresses himself for the fall and winter hunting, an ensemble that features the practicality of the old hunter and the dash of the cowboy. A ranchman, who usually dresses in flannel shirts and "overalls tucked into alligator boots," needs substantially heavier garments for cold weather and rough work: "there is nothing better than a fringed buckskin tunic or hunting-shirt (held in at the waist by the cartridge belt), buckskin trousers, and a fur cap, with heavy moccasins," together with fur gloves and a coonskin overcoat or jacket of fisher's fur for when the weather grows especially cold.

The American Museum of Natural History in New York displays one of Roosevelt's bespoke tunics, the sleeves lined with silk pinstripe and the chest ornamented with leather appliqués in the pattern of flowers (of all things); the tunic and matching trousers reveal him as a relatively small man, at least in his vigorous youth. For sleeping, he suggests a buffalo robe sewn up like a bag; when the temperature drops to sixty below zero, beaver robes and bearskins are warmest; for rainy days, an oilskin "slicker" and chaps keep the body dry.[28] For hunting on horseback, he selects "the best and most valuable animal on the ranch," named Manitou, a stout, strong, enduring, sure-footed, and fast horse. Before the hunt starts, he equips himself with a Winchester rifle, because "it is as deadly, accurate, and handy as any, stands very rough usage, and is unapproachable for the rapidity of its fire" (39). He also carries a 45 Colt or Smith & Wesson; and a hunter ought to have a couple of double-barreled shotguns, like his No. 10 choke-bore made by Thomas of Chicago and No. 16 hammerless by Kennedy of Saint Paul.

Roosevelt sets the stage for each hunt, much as he had set the stage for each battle in *The Naval War of 1812*, giving his reader precise details about equipment and weather and adversaries. Once equipped, the young hunter is ready for each episode as the book documents the shooting of specimens, the gutting of bodies, and preserving of heads and skins to authenticate his accomplishments as a hunter. The prizes he brought back adorned his house in Oyster Bay, and later filled the American Museum of Natural History in New York and, later still, the Smithsonian Museum in Washington, D.C., establishing him as game hunter and natural scientist.

The chapters are arranged not by the calendar of actual killings, but by the rarity of prey. Teal and wood ducks are relatively easy to shoot at lunchtime as the hungry hunters halt near ponds and reedy sloughs: "We had half an hour's good sport in 'jumping' these little ducks, moving cautiously along the margin of the reeds, keeping as much as possible concealed from view, and shooting four teal and a wood-duck, as, frightened, at our near approach, they sprang into the air and made off" (67). The truth is that the hunters are better than eagles at killing teals: "The little ducks went along like bullets; flop, flop came the great eagle after them," even as they dodged him by landing in the reeds (68). Roosevelt as a writer is very good at bringing the reader into the scene. As he walks along and hears a covey of prairie fowl, for example, he records "a loud kuk-kuk-kuk," growing into a "crowing cluck" if the birds are frightened, or settling into "a sociable garrulous cackling" when undisturbed. He trudges on foot in the fresh, cool morning air through a creek valley edged with "rose-bushes, bullberry bushes, ash, and wild cherry" thickets, taking shots along the way, nearly stepping on young grouse, and prizing himself for knowing where to aim as a bird takes flight, in order to kill it cleanly.

Deer are relatively hard to kill and muscular and for that reason had not been hunted to near extinction as were the buffalo and then the elk. Roosevelt puts himself into a hunting tale that begins with a wounding of a whitetail deer that leaves the animal limping on three legs but able to outrun and outsmart the hunters, who find his tracks and continue hunting the next morning, when the deer has weakened. "He turned his head sharply toward me," Roosevelt crowed, "as I raised the rifle, and the bullet went fairly into his throat, just under the jaw, breaking his neck, and bringing him down in his tracks with hardly a kick" (117).

The blacktail deer are larger, with two-pronged antlers, superior in every way to the "low-scudding, brush-loving white-tail" (137). They are regal: "Over rough ground, along precipitous slopes, and among the boulders of rocky cliffs, it will go with surprising rapidity and surefootedness, only surpassed by the feats of the big-horn in similar localities, and not equaled by those of any other plains game" (138). The blacktail are shy and scarce, requiring a hunter to go sure-footedly and quietly to be successful in seeing a buck, much less killing it. "Nevertheless, it is by still-hunting that most deer are killed, and the highest form of hunting craft is shown in the science of the skillful still-hunter" (143). And here, too, Roosevelt triumphs fifty pages later. He had been hunting mountain sheep, and as he "crept cautiously up to the edge of great gorge, whose sheer walls went straight down several hundred feet," he spied a blacktail buck lying on a narrow ledge. "He lay with his legs half stretched out, and his head turned so as to give me an exact centre-shot at his forehead; the bullet going in between his eyes, so that his legs hardly so much as twitched when he received it" (193). In his typical way, Roosevelt positions himself in a most difficult situation: "I have never known any other individual, even of this bold and adventurous species of deer, to take its noonday siesta in a place so barren of all cover and so difficult of access even to the most sure-footed climber" (193). He retrieves his prize, praising his own skills in completing the dangerous task.

The next chapter is on the antelope, and the artificiality of the book's structure is most apparent here for the simple reason that antelopes were actually his first kills at his Chimney Butte Ranch in June of 1884, only four months after Alice's death. In his diary, he flushes with pride: "I leaped off as they passed, within twenty five yards, and gave them both barrels, killing a fine buck shot through both shoulders."[29] Three days later, he rejoices over "the best shot I ever made with this rifle." The book version of the antelope hunt is colored by Roosevelt's sense of loss over the deaths of his wife and mother. It is a chapter more about landscape and loneliness than about heroic manliness as he travels on horseback to the west of the Badlands through the grand prairies in search of spiritual nourishment, the vast stretches of the American plains echoing the writer's mood. "Nowhere, not even at sea, does a man feel more lonely than when riding over the far-reaching, seemingly never-ending plains; and after a man has lived a little while on or near them, their very vastness and loneliness and their melancholy monotony have a strong fascination for him" (216). Nowhere else does a man feel so "far off from all mankind," Roosevelt confesses; "the plains stretch out in deathlike and measureless expanse." The landscape becomes for the lonely hunter almost a phantasm: "Although he can see so far, yet all objects on the outermost verge of the horizon, even though within the ken of his vision, look unreal and strange; for there is no shade to take away from the bright glare, and at a little distance things seem to shimmer and dance in the hot rays of the sun." At the distance of a mile, a white shape appears as a prairie wagon, but as the rider draws near, "it changes into the ghastly staring skull of some mighty buffalo, long dead and gone to join the rest of his vanished race" (217).

He admires the antelope, its care for the young, its capacity to be tamed and live almost as a pet, its battles with predatory eagles and wolves and coyotes. In the spirit of fair play, ranchmen have agreed to hunt antelopes only on horseback, and Roosevelt admits that they are so swift and unpredictable that he isn't much of a threat to them as a hunter. And yet, by the end of the essay, he leaps from his horse and aims perfectly. "An antelope's gait is so even that it offers a good running mark; and as the smoke blew off I saw the buck roll over like a rabbit, with both shoulders broken" (223). That kill is precisely the first that he recorded in his dairy on June 18. In the book, he re-created the scene, adding that he slit the throat and cut off the hams, and left the rest of the carcass because it offered so little meat. Not much practical use, finally, for this quarry.

His next kill is a bighorn ram, or mountain sheep, the hunting of which is what he calls the hardest kind of sport. In truth this hunt happened on December 14, 1884, and was the reason for his return to his Dakota ranch. In the book, he calls the chase "the noblest form of sport with the rifle" when it comes to an animal not dangerous to the hunter. The ram is rare and wary and next in size to the elk and buffalo. "The huge horns are carried proudly erect by the massive neck; and there seems to be no ground so difficult that the big-horn can not cross it" (246). It is comfortably at home in the vast, lonely, barren Badlands, camouflaged as a boulder. In the diary account Roosevelt records coming upon the ram and shooting him at ninety yards, but in the book the chase becomes riskier in the ice and snow. "Clambering instantly up the steep side, digging my hands and feet into the loose snow, and grasping at every little rock or frozen projection, I reached the top" (257). From his perch, he spots two rams; the bigger one, sturdy and massive against the sky, catches his eye. "I dropped to my knee, raising the rifle as I did so; for a second he did not quite make me out, turning his head half round to look." Roosevelt shoots him behind the shoulder, the bullet ranging clear through the body; even with such a death wound, the ram staggers and pitches and jumps and slides before his eyes roll up in death. A blizzard begins on his ride back to the Elkhorn ranch, and Roosevelt tells his reader, "I congratulated myself upon the last hunting trip I should take during that season" (259).

Roosevelt embroidered the story to keep his readers' attention. The buffalo hunt especially sounds like a yarn, perhaps because he wrote it from memory and not, as with the other kills, from diary notes. The plains buffalo had been hunted to extinction by "the rough forerunners of civilization" (7). It is a hard argument to make that the extinction of a noble animal somehow marks civilization, even harder that a sensitive naturalist would desire to shoot a "lordly" buffalo merely to fulfill his quest. Where is he to find such a creature in the first place? Cattle ranchers and hunters had changed the very nature of buffalo: "The formation of this race is due solely to the extremely severe process of natural selection that has been going on among the buffalo herds" (268). The ones that survived through adaptation are active and wary and suspicious, making them harder to find and kill. To find a buffalo, the men must lie flat on the ground and "wiggle like snakes" to avoid suspicion. "It was the first time I ever shot at buffalo," he admits, as he grazes the body with a loud crack, raising dust from the hide. The chase is on for the wounded bull over eight miles of rugged land, and even then Roosevelt misses the next shot. Mayhem ensues. "I tried to get in closer, when suddenly up went the bull's tail, and wheeling, he charged me with lowered horns" (284). Roosevelt's pony bolts, his rifle cracks against his forehead, blood flows into his eyes. Getting the better of the hunters, the bull vanishes. In a relatively wild and lonely spot, the hunters, hungry and thirsty, camp for the night, fearing that their horses might be stolen or, worse, that Indians might scalp them. Scared by wolves, the horses run off in the night, rain sets in, and the men cower, shivering under wet blankets.

In the morning, they find the horses and continue "over the formless, shapeless plain, all drenched through, and thoroughly uncomfortable" (287). Seeing before them a herd of buffalo, the men dismount and stalk their prey, slithering on hands and knees through the muddy terrain until they manage to get within shooting range. "To crown my misfortunes, I now made one of those misses which a man to his dying day always looks back upon with wonder and regret" (287). Stiff from the cold, numb in the fingers, sullen from the miss, Roosevelt continues to pursue the wily buffalo, and his yarn continues to stretch. Roosevelt claims that his pony hit a hole, turning a complete somersault and throwing him to the ground, and scrambled into a dry creek bed that gave way under the hooves, requiring the men to rescue the animal with ropes. Sunburned, parched, hungry, and cold, Roosevelt reminds his reader of an English proverb from *The Last Chronicle of Barset* by Anthony Trollope: "It's dogged as does it" (289). What other hunter would be thinking of a literary phrase from a British novelist at such a time? Peering over a hill, Roosevelt finally spots a great bull bison, trim and shining and lusty. "Before he could go off, I put the bullet in behind his shoulder," he beams. The hardest part for Roosevelt is cutting the trophy head off and stripping steaks from the carcass for dinner. When he returned to hunt in the fall of 1884, he lamented that even the wily buffalo were gone.

Roosevelt saw signs that the elk, called wapiti, were likewise disappearing because, ironically, their majestic bodies made them desirable and conspicuous to hunters. He had seen for himself the results of the slaughter over his short years along the Little Missouri River. The elk, already chased from New York, Pennsylvania, Virginia, Kentucky, and Tennessee, had abandoned the plains for the protection of dense woods in the Rocky Mountains. "The last individual of the race," Roosevelt records in a strange echo of James Fenimore Cooper's Mohicans, "was killed in the Adirondacks in 1834; in Pennsylvania not till nearly thirty years later; while a very few are still to be found in northern Michigan." He deplores the relentless persecution, even extermination, of the stately creature. The movement of European settlers across the United States, the very Manifest Destiny that Roosevelt chronicled and admired, threatened the natural world he loved.

The young man, a naïve narrator, fails to grasp the irony. "The gradual extermination of this, the most stately and beautiful animal of the chase to be found in America, can be looked upon only with unmixed regret by every sportsman and lover of nature" (296). This is, after all, a book about hunting. His central question is how the sportsman will find an elk to kill after they are all gone. For Roosevelt, the place to go is farther west to the Bighorn Mountains, where intrepid hunters had not yet prevailed. "I have had very good sport with them in a still wilder and more western region; and this I will now describe," he promises his reader (297). Eventually, Roosevelt manages to kill his prey. "I only brought down one elk, a full-grown cow, with a broken neck, dead in its tracks," he reports, "but I also broke the hind leg of a bull calf" (304). His diary records the same shot on September 6, 1884: "killed an old cow and a bull calf as they ran off." In the book, he gives flesh to the scene: "They look very handsome as they trot through the wood, stepping lightly and easily over the dead trunks and crashing through the underbrush, with the head held up and nose pointing forward" (304).

Roosevelt is good at taking his reader into the scene. "All of the sights and sounds in these pine woods that clothed the Bighorn Mountains reminded me of the similar ones seen and heard in the great, somber forests of Maine and the Adirondacks" (308). He is especially good when he stops to listen, noting a "nutcracker, a large, noisy, crow-like bird, with many of the habits of a woodpecker," and "a Little Chief hare, a wee animal, with a shrill, timorous squeak." Gazing on the natural world, he ponders its meaning. "The great pine-clad mountains, their forests studded with open glades, were the best place for the still-hunter's craft. Going noiselessly through them in our dull-colored buckskin and noiseless moccasins, we kept getting glimpses, as it were, of the inner life of the mountains. Each animal that we saw had its own individuality. Aside from the thrill and tingle that a hunter experiences at the sight of his game, I by degrees grew to feel as if I had a personal interest in the different traits and habits of the wild creatures" (314).

His last quarry is the grizzly bear. "The lumbering, self-confident gait of the bears, their burly strength, and their half-humorous, half-ferocious look, gave me a real insight into their character," he confides, "and I never was more impressed by the exhibition of vast, physical power, than when watching from an ambush a grisly burying or covering up an elk carcass" (314–15). The grizzly bear was the closest beast he could find in North America to rival his sibling Elliott's tigers in India. "Still, after all is said, the man should have a thoroughly trustworthy weapon and a fairly cool head who would follow into his own haunts and slay grim Old Ephraim" (326). Old Ephraim is a legendary name for grizzlies of prodigious size and ferocity; Roosevelt's grizzly was, in truth, not large or particularly fearsome. The story of the bear hunt began in his diary when he, clad in moccasins, followed a trail "noiselessly up, and found him in his bed. I shot him through the brain at 25 feet," he reported on September 16, 1884. From his notes, Roosevelt built the ultimate tale of hunting in the West. The story has a good deal of color, complete with anecdotes about the danger of bears to humans and to other animals, including elk. In the scene itself, Roosevelt strides past his partner Merrifield with his rifle ready as the bear rears up from his bed, stands on his haunches to fight, and drops back bristling on all fours, sensing the danger before him. He personalizes the battle: "And when I saw the top of the white head fairly between his small, glittering, evil eyes, I pulled the trigger" (338). How did the eyes come to glitter? How is it that Old Ephraim is evil? In the contest, Roosevelt claims both bravery and skill in firing a single shot between the eyes "as if the distance had been measured by a carpenter's rule," the whole thing over in twenty seconds. The speller in Roosevelt could not resist stopping the story to talk about the pun on "grisly," meaning horrible, and "grizzly," the conventional spelling, from "grizzled," meaning fur tinged with gray color (339). And he ends the story, indeed the collection, with an anecdote about a grizzly that broke the skull and gnawed the arm of a hunter.

The book is experimental and fragmentary, dwelling on episodes in the life of a naturalist and hunter. G. P. Putnam's Sons contracted with the young writer to publish five hundred copies, called the Medora Edition — after the town of Medora, where Roosevelt's ranch was located — bound in canvas and gold lettering, printed on large-size, handwoven paper, and illustrated with stunning works of art. At the same time, they printed one thousand copies of a popular edition and agreed to print more if sales were good. Roosevelt agreed to pay $5,000 ($120,000 in today's dollars) up front with any other expenses to follow and would own the plates himself. The press agreed to pay him 65 percent of the large paper edition, 50 percent of the popular one, and 75 percent of any sales in foreign countries; payments were to come twice a year in February and August. The Medora volume cost fifteen dollars (over $350 today), and one wonders what audience he had in mind. "The book is far too sumptuous for the general public," sniffed a reviewer in the *Athenaeum*.[30]

The *New York Times* signaled approval of its hometown writer: "Mr. Roosevelt writes most happily, tells naturally what he sees and does, and 'Hunting Trips of a Ranchman' will take a leading position in the literature of the American sportsman."[31] No review would ever be as crisp and true about Theodore Roosevelt's prose. Another laudatory piece in the *Saturday Review* on August 29, 1885, ranked the book in the top ten of "sporting classics" of western literature. Editions followed in the United States and Britain, earning favorable reviews on both sides of the Atlantic.

George Bird Grinnell, editor and reviewer of *Forest and Stream*, took the young writer to task: "Where Mr. Roosevelt details his own adventures he is accurate, and tells his story in a simple, pleasant fashion," he began, offering the caveat "that hunting myths are given as fact," owing to the author's inexperience. He joked good-naturedly: "A man who went gunnin' or fishin' lost caste among respectable people just about in the same way that one did who got drunk."[32] Roosevelt, an instinctive politician, had a way of absorbing criticism. He would work with Grinnell to found the Boone and Crockett Club and coauthor *American Big-Game Hunting* and *Hunting in Many Lands*.

In London, the *Spectator* hailed the young writer: "What Harte has done for the miners Theodore Roosevelt has done for the more manlier and useful folk of the plains, the ranchmen and cowboys."[33] Roosevelt understood the gravity of the comparison. He admired Harte's stories, including "The Outcasts of Poker Flat," and thrilled to the sounds in his Civil War poetry, selecting "The Reveille" as epigraph to *The Rough Riders*: "Hark! I hear the tramp of thousands/And of armed men the hum." When Bret Harte died in 1902, President Roosevelt congratulated California on giving us "so great a figure in our literary development." Reading such reviews, Theodore Roosevelt knew that he, too, was taking his place in American letters.

Chapter 4
Chasing Desperadoes

Writing is horribly hard work for me; and I make slow progress.
I have got some good ideas in the first chapter, but I am not sure
they are worked up rightly; my style is very rough and I do not like
a certain lack of sequitur that I do not seem able to get rid of.
{ Theodore Roosevelt to Henry Cabot Lodge, March 27, 1886 }

I like it: he gets pretty near the truth. He don't write it
exactly as I would, of course: that's because he don't enter
into it — puts on his glasses before he looks at it — writes it with
a little the touch of a dude. Still, there is something alluring in
the subject and the way it is handled: Roosevelt seems to have
realized its character — its shape and size — to have honestly
imbibed some of the spirit of that wild Western life.
{ Walt Whitman to Horace Traubel, October 1, 1888 }[1]

Three men had the misfortune to steal a boat from Theodore Roosevelt's Elkhorn Ranch in the early spring thaw of 1886, as the ice began to break up on the Little Missouri River, allowing them to escape local vigilantes, known as "stranglers," who already suspected them of horse stealing and had them in their sights. The stolen boat was clinker-built with overlapping planks along the hull, making the vessel light and fast (the design of Viking ships). Roosevelt knew the value of his boat and wanted it back. Even as he chased the thieves, he imagined telling the story, packing a camera and a diary. Sparse lines in this diary and embellishments in letters back home grew over several months into "Sheriff's Work on a Ranch," an article for *Century Magazine*, and then into a chapter in Roosevelt's second book on the Dakotas, *Ranch Life and the Hunting-Trail* (1888).

The *Century* sketch places both writer and reader in the middle of the action. The Little Missouri, as he describes it, is typical of rivers on the plains, at times dwindling and sluggish and then, at the next bend, torrential and shifting. The river "rises and falls with extraordinary suddenness and intensity; an instance of which has just occurred as this very page is being written."[2] He wants us to believe that he is writing in the moment, crafting language as the action unfolds. The idea of writing along the way is at the heart of his hunting stories, and later in Africa and Brazil, he would, in truth, take paper tablets with him and devote evening hours to his life as a writer. In the Dakotas he was writing in his diary most days, merely listing rough details.

Medora seemed to Roosevelt emblematic of the struggle to end the lawlessness of the frontier days. These thieves "belonged to a class that always holds sway during the raw youth of a frontier community, and the putting down of which is the first step towards decent government," the historian schooled his readers. In his local role as volunteer deputy sheriff, the young scion of the Roosevelt family was casting himself as a decent force in the change from raw frontier to civilization. The three characters on the run were suspicious types, what he called "white desperadoes," including the leader, a man named Finnigan "who had long red hair reaching to his shoulders," and his accomplices, a stout, muscular "half-breed" named Bernstead and a "weak and shiftless" German named Wharfenberger (115).

Much of the rhetoric that would characterize Theodore Roosevelt as a writer and a politician can be found in this early ranch tale. He insists, "To submit tamely and meekly to theft, or to any other injury, is to invite almost certain repetition of the offense, in a place where self-reliant hardihood and the ability to hold one's own under all circumstances rank as the first of virtues" (115). His later political and military doctrines would be based on the logic of holding one's own. He credits the ranchers Sewall and Dow with possessing certain animal traits: "They were tough, hardy, resolute fellows, quick as cats, strong as bears, and able to travel like bull moose" (116). In his fuller portrait of manly heroism, the male is like an animal—cat, bear, bull moose—the last simile rooted firmly in Roosevelt's imagination. As always, he suits up his heroes. The Elkhorn ranchers set off on the thief hunt in a "holiday" mood, dressed warmly in "woolen socks and underclothes, heavy jackets and trousers, and great fur coats," carrying rifles and double-barreled duck guns for the pleasure of sport and delight of dinner.

The surprise for everyone along the Little Missouri River in the ice melt that year was the mercurial nature of the weather, warming early in late February only to freeze hard again in a spring blizzard. The ferocity

of the wind and the chill of the temperature were harbingers of the cat-
aclysmic blizzard to come in the next winter, a storm that would change
the nature of cattle ranching in the Dakotas. The spring journey down the
river through the alluvial valley bordered by great barren buttes, blotched
in vivid colors of clay and marl and sandstone, seemed to the young writer
fantastical, terrible, and grotesque. The world around him glistened
weirdly in the twilight, uncouth, grim, and forbidding. He struggled to
find the right language to evoke the mood of Dakotan desolation, quoting from memory the mythically dense lines of his favorite poet, Robert
Browning, in "Childe Roland to the Dark Tower Came."

> Those two hills on the right
> Crouched like two bulls locked horn in horn in fight —
> While to the left a tall scalped mountain. . . .
> The dying sunset kindled through a cleft:
> The hills, like giants at a hunting, lay
> Chin upon hand, to see the game at bay —

A "childe" himself—the medieval term for an untested knight—Theodore
Roosevelt called on his poetic memory and that of his reader to depict
himself as a novice in the tale, like Roland, not yet a fledged hero.

On the third day, they rowed around a bend to discover the empty
clinker boat tied on shore alongside a leaky scow belonging to the thieves.
As the men pulled up, Roosevelt described the thrill and tingle in the
blood, only to admit that the actual encounter was "as tame as possible,"
as with guns drawn they surprised the German who was tending the fire
by himself. He did not put up a fight at all, nor did the other two when
they returned to face Roosevelt's rifle. The mundane task of delivering the
thieves to justice was to take several days in an unrelenting blizzard with
three more mouths to feed and bodies to keep warm.

How did they spend their time? "If the time was tedious to us," Roosevelt explained, "it must have seemed never-ending to our prisoners, who
had nothing to do but to lie still and read, or chew the bitter cud of their
reflections" (126). So the desperadoes were readers? It turned out they
packed "quite a stock of books," including an expected collection of dime
novels, the *History of the James Brothers*, and copies of the *Police Ga-
zette*, together with a large bundle of unexpected "silly 'society'" novels by
Ouida, the Duchess, and Augusta J. Evans. Maria Louise Ramé, an exotic
literary figure, wrote under the pen name Ouida and belonged to a literary salon that included Robert Browning, together with more decadent

figures, including Oscar Wilde and Algernon Swinburne. She wrote sensational, romantic novels, including *Under Two Flags*, that championed imperialism and would seem, by any measure, a cheeky choice for common criminals. The Duchess was the American pen name of Margaret Hamilton, an Irish novelist who wrote popular romantic fiction. The best novelist in the collection was Augusta Jane Evans, a beloved southern writer, whose books sold in the millions in both the South and the North as she used her pen to depict and promote Confederate ideals. The thieves carried their library with them to "greedily devour" on lonely, dull days in the West. Biographers have thought Roosevelt borrowed the James biography to read himself, but the truth is that he was such an eclectic reader that he probably had already read the book. The library collection looks suspiciously like books the Roosevelt children grew up on, and that may be how he came up with the list as he embellished the tale for *Century Magazine*.

In the later version, published in *Ranch Life and the Hunting-Trail*, Roosevelt admitted that while the robbers devoured their books, he was actually reading Leo Tolstoy's *Anna Karenina*: "My surroundings were quite gray enough to harmonize well with Tolstoi." And he told Cabot Lodge that he was packing Matthew Arnold's *Discourses in America* but had not yet found a chance to read it.

The flotilla of men and boats finally found themselves at the end of the ice jam in front of a neighbor's camp. Sewall and Dow took the boats back to the Elkhorn Ranch, while Roosevelt performed the lone task of squiring the thieves to the jail in Dickinson. He hired a prairie schooner and driver, who looked skeptically on the idea of carrying the men to justice when simply hanging them seemed justice enough. Roosevelt boasted that he completed his task on "a gloomy walk" behind the wagon, staying awake for the thirty-six-hour journey. "Hour after hour went by always the same, while I plodded along through the dreary landscape—hunger, cold, and fatigue struggling with a sense of dogged, weary resolution" (128). The story ended when Roosevelt, as a volunteer sheriff, walked the thieves into town and to the jail.

Crafting the tale for *Century*, the writer told the truth, mainly. In his diary for 1886, he had sketched a skeleton of the story that would swell over the course of its retelling. He started for Medora on March 15, 1886, to spend the summer "on my little ranch."[3] Most days, he simply recorded his kills—deer, mountain lions, prairie chickens—the size of his prey and the distance of the shot. Nine days into his trip on Wednesday, March

24, he mentioned matter-of-factly, "thieves stole boat." It took Sewall and Dow two days to build the scow to go after them, but then they were stalled by the weather, making it too cold to start for three more days. The diary charted conditions: "River very high; ice piled up on banks several feet"; "Bitter cold"; "Furious blizzard." Not until the Tuesday after the theft could the men set out to capture the thieves, a hunt that took two days. By Thursday, April 1, Roosevelt noted, almost in passing, "Shot white tail doe (75 yards); Dow shot another. Captured the three boat thieves." Over the next five days he jotted down phrases, "hung up by ice" and "jam again stopped us." By Wednesday, April 7, they had worked their way out of the tails of the ice floe and arrived at a camp of the neighboring C Diamond Ranch, shooting two prairie chickens along the way. The rest of his mission to hire a wagon and take the captives to Dickinson took five days. In the diary account, Roosevelt rode to Kildeer Mountain to hire a wagon on Thursday; walked the captives there on Friday; drove them in the wagon to Captain Brown's ranch on Saturday; and, finally, delivered the captives to the sheriff in Dickinson on Sunday. Returning to Medora on Monday, April 12, Roosevelt went back to the business of cattle ranching in preparation for a stock meeting. He didn't have much, yet, to build a story on.

What Theodore Roosevelt didn't tell his *Century* readers is a more scintillating tale. One thing he was shy talking about, even in his letters to Corinne, was his inner struggle with the moral obligation to his dead wife Alice, Reverend Hall's admonition about "groveling passions," and the "precious and present and blessed hope" of a heavenly reunion much in his mind. The young father had been shattered by the loss, but over a year had passed, and he strongly desired Edith Carow, the childhood friend he had pined for while traveling with his family in Europe and flirted and fought with in college before he met Alice. In the fall of 1885, the romance had rekindled when Theodore returned to New York in September to help in the gubernatorial campaign and ran into Edith at his sister's house.[4] He stayed on to heal an arm he had broken in a Meadowbrook hunt on October 26, and it didn't take long — November 17 — for him to propose, giving Edith a ring, a watch, and a pearl necklace. They agreed to keep the engagement secret until the end of 1886, observing a customary two years and more of mourning. As the lovers waited, he took a train west to the Dakotas and she a ship east with her mother and sister, who were moving to England because it was less expensive to live abroad on the modest inheritance from Edith's father.

She was an avid reader and letter writer, but also a private woman, who saved only one of her love letters (June 8, 1886) to Theodore during their engagement. Reading it, we see what a splendidly candid writer Edith was: "You know I love you very much and would do anything in the world to please you. I wish I could be sure my letters sound as much like myself as yours do like you. You know all about me darling. I never could have loved anyone else. I love you with all the passion of a girl who has never loved before, and please be patient with me when I cannot put my heart on paper."

We may know more about their passion and patience from a letter that Theodore later wrote from Africa (November 12, 1909), marking the twenty-third anniversary of their engagement, when he lovingly teased: "Do you remember when you were such a pretty engaged girl and said to your lover 'no Theodore, that I cannot allow?'"[5] They waited out the time thousands of miles apart.

In the fall of 1886, the *New York Times* got wind of gossip and announced their engagement in the social column. Theodore wrote sheepishly to Anna on September 20 about his failure to give her the news, describing himself as savagely irritated: "I utterly disbelieve in and disapprove of second marriages; I have always considered that they argued weakness in a man's character. You could not reproach me one half as bitterly for my inconstancy and faithlessness, as I reproach myself. Were I sure there were a heaven my one prayer would be I might never go there, lest I should meet those I love on earth who are dead."[6]

He described the early college romance with Edith and its rupture, "for we both of us had, and I suppose have, tempers that were far from being the best." Behind their tempers was a forceful passion that lay in the background of the icy chase after desperadoes, as Theodore, huddled under furs, read *Anna Karenina*.

Another thing that Roosevelt didn't mention in his *Century* article was his desire, especially with a new wife and family in his future, to earn money as a writer. He had completed a series of hunting stories for the sporting magazine *Outing*, where his "Ranch-Life and Game-Hunting in the West" was the lead article in March 1886.[7]

Newspaper reporters picked up the *Outing* articles and suspected that Roosevelt was acting as both writer and publisher. The magazine's founder and editor, Poultney Bigelow, wrote in "Editor's Open Window" that he regretted a misapprehension about control of the magazine: "No financial or executive responsibility whatsoever attaches to Mr. Theodore

Roosevelt."[8] The note was made by the request of the author, irritated by any hint of literary collusion as he worked to establish himself as a credible historian.

Only in his letters does he talk about his life as a historian. Waiting for Sewall and Dow to build the scow and "all snowed up by a blizzard," the young writer was struggling with a second academic book![9] His biography of Missouri senator Thomas Hart Benton was to appear in the Houghton Mifflin's American Statesmen series, an impressive project that would grow over the years into forty volumes, four of them written by Roosevelt's close friend Henry Cabot Lodge (*George Washington*, parts 1 and 2, *Alexander Hamilton*, and *Daniel Webster*) and two by Roosevelt, *Thomas Hart Benton* and *Gouverneur Morris*. He confessed to Lodge that writing the Benton book was daunting: "I have written the first chapter of the Benton; so at any rate I have made a start. Writing is horribly hard work for me; and I make slow progress. I have got some good ideas in the first chapter, but I am not sure they are worked up rightly; my style is very rough and I do not like a certain lack of sequitur that I do not seem able to get rid of." With Lodge, he could be painfully direct, utterly without pretense.

Nor did Roosevelt's western tale tell the story of his early political life in New York, where he had had the distinction, at twenty-three years of age in November 1881, of being the youngest New York assemblyman ever to be elected, and where he had become an irritant to party bosses on both sides of the aisle. He was reelected twice, serving also as a delegate to the Republican National Convention in Chicago in 1884. His letters to Lodge record his testing of political waters in the East amid doubts that he had a future in American politics. He mused about chances that a war might break out over a border incident with Mexico, giving him the chance for some feat, "*qua* cowboy, not *qua* statesman," a reason to organize "an utterly reckless . . . set of desperadoes" as a volunteer regiment in the war (an idea that would come to fruition in Cuba in 1898 and to haunt him as the Great War erupted in Europe in 1914). "It is no use saying that I would like a chance at something I thought I could really do." He confessed, "At present I see nothing whatever ahead."[10]

The Elkhorn chase offered the young writer — *qua* cowboy, *qua* sheriff — a tale of real desperadoes. On April 12, 1886, the day he returned to the Elkhorn Ranch from the adventure with the boat thieves, he wrote Elliot and Corinne versions of the story. To his brother, he gave particulars, but the letter to Corinne indulged in brotherly whining: "I have been absent just a fortnight. It has been very rough work, as we got entirely out of

THEODORE ROOSEVELT

food and had an awful time in the river, as there were great ice gorges, the cold being intense. We captured the three men by surprise, there being no danger or difficulty about it whatever, as it turned out; and the last ten days I have hung to them, through good and evil fortune, like a fate, rifle always in hand." Yet he bragged, "I was pretty well done out with the work, the lack of sleep and the strain of the constant watchfulness, but I am as brown and as tough as a pine knot and feel equal to anything."[11]

What Theodore really wanted to talk to Corinne about was the novel he had been reading. As Sewall and Dow fought the ice floes with paddles and poles and the temperature hung at zero, the young man sat in the middle of the scow reading his English translation of *Anna Karenina*. "I took Anna Karenina along on the trip and have read it through with very great interest. I hardly know whether to call it a very bad book or not." Tolstoy may be a great writer, he reflected, because the novel was unmoral rather than immoral. Roosevelt would spend much of his life quarreling in letters and essays about the moral nature of Tolstoy's prose as well as his politics, but at that moment he "was much pleased with the insight into Russian life." Anyone who knew Theodore Roosevelt would assume that the focus of his attention would be Konstantin Dmitrievich Levin and his struggle to achieve a valid life. A line like "the idea came into [Levin's] mind that it was in his power to exchange the onerous, idle, artificial, and selfish existence he was leading for that busy, honourable, delightful life of common toil" should have resonated in Roosevelt's young mind as he considered similar choices in his own life.[12] And yet he considered Levin and Kitty's story a mere subplot, he told his sister, that "need not have existed at all" in the novel.

His mind fixed on Anna Karenina's sexual attraction and attraction to sex. Her "groveling passions" unnerved the young man: "She is portrayed as being a prey to the most violent passion and subject to melancholia, and her reasonning power is so unbalanced that she could not possibly be described otherwise than as in a certain sense insane." In the bottom of the scow, huddled in furs, in the midst of a blizzard, chasing desperadoes, Roosevelt himself might have been feeling a bit insane as he read Anna's musings: "'Where was it I left off? On the reflection that I couldn't conceive a situation in which life would not be a misery, that we were all created in order to suffer, and that we all know this and all try to invent means for deceiving ourselves. But when you see the truth, what are you to do?'" Tolstoy's Anna put that question to Theodore at a time when he thought he had put misery and suffering behind him.

He hoped for a future with Edith Carow that would allow moral expression of groveling passions. He prodded Corinne for news about Edith without a word of their engagement. When would she be leaving for Europe? Could Corinne send her a gift from him to mark the voyage? "I suppose fruit would be more useful, but I think flowers 'more tenderer.'" The brave soul who thought he was as "tough as a pine knot" had a soft side that his ranch tales worked to hide. Three days later, on April 15, 1886, he wrote his sister again; at the bottom of the page, seemingly as an afterthought, he wrote, "I enclose a card to send with the flowers to Edith when she starts off."[13] And in a postscript, he asked his sister to express mail him "three or four cakes of that nice transparent soap." The rugged Theodore had taken a bathtub with him to Medora and relished the smell and comfort of a sybaritic rite. A month later, he thanked her: "I am very much obliged to you, sweet Pussie, for the soap; it was just what I needed."[14]

Roosevelt told Lodge the story of chasing desperadoes in a single paragraph. "I got the three horsethieves in fine style. My two Maine men and I ran down the river three days in our boat and then came on their camp by surprise. As they knew there was no other boat on the river but the one they had taken and as they had not thought of our building another they were taken completely unawares, one with his rifle on the ground, and the others with theirs on their shoulders; so there was no fight, nor any need of pluck on our part."[15] No need of pluck. The story, at this point, was only a few sentences long. The letters ends with the boast: "I am as brown and as tough as a hickory nut now."

He turned his pen to his sister Anna, whose interests lay, along with his, in the arts and humanities, and who had just returned from a tour of Mexico. Theodore joked fondly with her about their lifetime goal of organizing a literary salon, the one the Roosevelt children had begun in Dresden with the motto "We Are No Asses." As playful as the idea seemed, he would work in earnest much later as president to gather around him at the White House the sort of group she had in mind. Theodore hoped that Anna's friends in Mexico would help them in building an international literary circle, "that far distant salon wherein we are to gather society men who take part in politics, literature and art and politicians, authors and artists whose bringing up and personal habits do not disqualify them for society; where the clever women will neither dress too prismatically nor yet have committed the still graver crime of marrying dull husbands and where the pretty women who know how to dress and dance will not have brains of those of Gussie Drayton and Mamie Astor."[16]

His letters to Anna are witty in ways that remind us that he grew up alongside Edith "Pussy" Jones Wharton, both of them eying the absurdities of wealth in Old New York. The novelist was related distantly to Edith Carow and would remain close in spirit to Theodore without often being in his company. The two brilliant and rebellious Old New York writers saw the world in much the same way. The letter to Anna is a delight for anyone who has read Wharton's *The House of Mirth*, *The Custom of the Country*, and most especially *The Age of Innocence*. The second paragraph begins with a line that would have charmed Wharton: "Why is it that even such of our friends as do things that sound interesting do them in a way that makes them very dull?" The comment that follows neatly catches his derision. "The Beckmans are two fine looking fellows of excellent family and faultless breeding, with a fine old country place, four in hands, tandems, a yacht and so on; but, oh, the decorous hopelessness of their lives!" "Decorous hopelessness" was precisely Wharton's critique of the American rich, and Roosevelt had come west that year to escape such hopelessness in his own life.

"I enjoy my life at present," he confided to Anna in May. "I have my time fully occupied with work of which I am fond; and so have none of my usual restless, caged wolf feeling."[17] Restlessness, the feeling of being caged, would follow Theodore Roosevelt throughout his life. He found life in Medora curative, filled as it was with hunting, ranching, and writing.

The letters give us a clear sense of Roosevelt's habits as a writer at his Elkhorn ranch. "I have managed to combine an outdoors life, possessing much variety and excitement and now and then a little adventure, with a literary life also. Three out of four days I spend the morning and evening in the ranch house," he wrote Corinne, "where I have a sitting room all to myself, reading and working at various pieces I have now on hand. They may come to nothing whatever; but on the other hand they may succeed; at any rate I am doing some honest work, whatever the result is. I am really pretty philosophical about success and failure now."[18] As he put it to Anna, "I hunt, ride and lead the wild, half adventurous life of a ranchman."[19]

With Lodge, he kept his eye on the political terrain, but professed, "Really, I enjoy this life; with books, guns and horses, and this free, open air existence."[20] He sent news that Richard Watson Gilder, editor of *Century Magazine*, had asked for the story of the boat thief hunt: "I don't know whether to write it or not." The biography of Benton was half written, and he promised to send it to the series editor John Torrey Morse in a fortnight. He was leaving for the spring roundup in late May and hoped "to snatch a day or two" in order to finish the manuscript by the end of June. "I have really become interested in it; but I can not tell whether what I have done is worth anything or not." He thought Lodge's book on Daniel Webster was good; in a display of writer envy, Theodore groused that Benton was simply "not as good a subject."[21]

Seventeen days later, he told Lodge he was in a literary jam: "I wonder if your friendship will stand a very serious strain. I have pretty nearly finished Benton, mainly evolving him from my inner consciousness."[22] "Inner consciousness" comes perilously close to imaginative play, the stuff of fiction. The book was moving very quickly toward the desired eighty thousand words, but the author admitted that he knew "nothing whatever" about Benton's life after his subject left the Senate in 1850. "Being by nature both a timid and, on occasions, by choice a truthful man," he joked, "I would prefer to have some foundation of fact, no matter how slender, on which to build the airy and arabesque superstructure of my fancy—especially as I am writing a history." He drew the line at providing a fictional date for Benton's death and asked Lodge to hire a copyist who could look up a handful of facts he could use to complete the manuscript. Medora gave him time to write but was no place for a scholar.

His history was indeed airy and arabesque. Thomas Hart Benson did not arrive in his own biography until page twelve, and even then only as a walk-on, listed merely as "Benton in Missouri." The putative hero of the book, Roosevelt explained, had not shaped events already under way in the country: "Benton was not one of the few statesmen who have left the indelible marks of their own individuality upon our history; but he was, perhaps, the most typical representative of the statesmanship of the Middle West at the time when the latter gave the tone to the political thought of the entire Mississippi valley."[23] Benton was a leader who paid small heed to the "refined, graceful, and cultivated statesmanship" of the East Coast and who favored "men of abounding vitality, of rugged intellect and of indomitable will" from the Middle West. Roosevelt gave him that credit: "No better or more characteristic possessor of these attributes could be imagined than Thomas Benton" (22). By the end of the first chapter, the senator took his place in the story. We discover that he held slaves, sided with the South on issues of slavery in new states, favored the removal of Indian tribes from the South and West to make way for "civilization," argued for the westward expansion of American territory, struggled to give land outright to white settlers, opposed the spoils system in civil service, and believed in hard currency. Over his thirty years in the Senate, he was racist, grim, rigid, determined, and "unfortunately deficient in sense of humor" (52).

Roosevelt used the very language of Benton's speeches, interlarded with pretentious references to the Roman Empire, to poke fun. Another Benton hobbyhorse was "the iniquity of taxing salt," an issue he would squeeze into any speech on the floor of the Senate; not surprisingly, "his associates, unless of a humorous turn of mind," found his tirades tiresome. As with senators in any period, quoting them verbatim offered the best chance at humor, and Roosevelt was good at this. In a speech about commerce on the Mississippi, for example, Benton alluded to New Orleans as "that great city which revives upon the banks of the Mississippi the name of the greatest of the emperors [Aurelian] that ever reigned upon the banks of the Tiber, and who eclipsed the glory of his own heroic exploits by giving an order to his legions never to levy a contribution of salt upon a Roman citizen!" (93). American humor doesn't get much better. Another of Benton's hobbies was opposition to the presidential veto. Roosevelt quipped, "When on his ultra-democratic hobby Benton always rode very loose in the saddle, and with little knowledge of where he was going" (128).

Much of the biography itself was written "very loose in the saddle," suggesting it was not necessarily about Thomas Hart Benton himself but rather about the geographical and political terrain in Roosevelt's mind at the time. Benton had, he concluded, "the tenacity of a snapping turtle" (225–26). "His tenacity and his pertinacious refusal to abandon any contest, no matter what the odds were against him, and no matter how often he had to return to the charge, formed two of his most invaluable qualities, and when called into play on behalf of such an object as the preservation of the Union, cannot receive too high praise at our hands." The snapping turtle might serve as a comic image of Roosevelt himself, and many readers over the years have seen the Benton book as autobiography of a sort. "I feel a little appalled over the Benton," he admitted to Lodge; "I have not the least idea whether I shall make a flat failure of it or not."[24] In characteristic fashion, he shook off doubt: "However I will do my best and trust to luck for the result."

Theodore talked in code with Lodge, who could follow his rapid shifts of thought. After the roundup that summer on June 7, he enthused, "It has been great fun; but hard work — fourteen to sixteen hours every day. Breakfast comes at three; and I am pretty sleepy, all the time."[25] And, then, just as enthusiastically, he shifted to take issue with Robert Browning's poem "Another Way of Love." "That intellectual prank can't be even parsed, much less understood. It isn't obscure, it's unintelligible." He ended the letter by promising Lodge's wife, Nannie, that he intended to "make a serious study of the gentleman from Avon [Shakespeare]."

The truth is that he was seriously studying Tolstoy, reading *War and Peace* in French and ranting to Anna that the novel proved the author's moral weakness: "Moreover when he criticizes battles (and the iniquity of war) in his capacity of author, he deprives himself of all excuse for the failure to criticize the various other immoralities he portrays."[26] Anna Karenina was still much on the young man's mind. If the great novelist spent pages "descanting on the wickedness and folly of war," why hadn't he likewise probed Anna's sexual depravity? Still, he found "touches and descriptions that are simply masterpieces."

On his own literary efforts, he reported: "I write steadily three or four days, and then hunt." His pen shifted back and forth between the story of the boat chase and the history of Benton. Much of his inheritance had gone into the Elkhorn ranch, with little to show for his investment. Consequently, he was writing that summer to earn money to go hunting in the Rockies, because to afford the trip in July, he would need to publish something, or else he would have to borrow money. The Benton book had stalled because he needed to work in the Astor Library in New York City to square his story with actual documents, and the manuscript would not, therefore, earn the expected $500 (he had thirty pages left to write).

The thief-hunting story would provide cash, but he had run into resistance from Anna and Cabot Lodge, both of whom were reading drafts. Letters in late June hint at the problem. To Anna he wrote, "As both you and Cabot advise so strongly against sending in the horse thief piece to the Century I suppose I shall keep that too, though I do not quite see why it would be better to have it incorporated in anything else; of course I shall take good care that the pronoun 'I' does not appear once in the whole piece, if it can possibly be avoided."[27] In brotherly pique, he added, "One minor result of my not sending in these various pieces will be to prevent my going to the Rockies, as, on several accounts, I do not wish to draw any money from Douglas this summer if by any chance it can be helped." One cannot help but note that "I" appeared twenty-seven times in the very letter he was writing to her about the problem, four times in the sentence of the promise itself. And later that same day, Theodore wrote his brother-in-law Douglas Robinson asking for advice, since it was his money that Roosevelt would need to borrow, about the fact that Anna and Cabot

Lodge had both advised against the *Century* publication. "I suppose they think it would look egotistical. What do you think?"[28] A good question.

The story stressed Roosevelt's hardihood and strength and bravery, the very myth that would continue to grow from his pen over the years. The final version of the story, published as a chapter in the ranching book, included only six of the offending "I"s. Maybe to assuage his ego, he attached a letter to the story, purportedly written from prison by Finnigan, who apologized for the theft of the boat in a fairly literate paragraph that managed to stuff twenty-one "I"s into a brief space. Sounding suspiciously like Roosevelt himself, Finnigan enthuses, "I have read a good many of your sketches of ranch life in the papers since I have been here, and they interest me deeply."

Perhaps the man who loved his stories most was the Harvard English professor Hermann Hagedorn, who wrote *Theodore Roosevelt* (1918), followed by *Roosevelt in the Badlands* (1921). Hagedorn's version of the boat-theft story includes accounts of contemporary locals, including "Dickinson Letter to the Newburyport *Herald*," a newspaper column published in Massachusetts.[29] The *Herald* columnist was astonished to find a New Yorker "masquerading in the character of an impromptu sheriff," dressed in a cowboy's hat, corduroy jacket, flannel shirt, and heavy shoes, and roaring: "'I don't know how I look, but I feel first-rate!'" The doctor in Medora who had treated Roosevelt that Sunday morning told Hagedorn, "He did not seem worn out or unduly tired. . . . He had just come from the jail, having deposited his prisoners at last, and had had no sleep for forty-eight hours, and he was all teeth and eyes; but even so he seemed a man unusually wide awake." The portrait, all teeth and eyes, wide-awake, is spot on. The doctor added a simile that many of Roosevelt's friends used affectionately: "He was just like a boy." The best line came from a fellow rancher John Simpson, who gibed, "Roosevelt, no one but you would have followed those men with just a couple of cow-hands. You are the only real damned fool in the county."

"Sheriff's Work on a Ranch" did not appear until May 1888 in *Century Magazine* as an installment in a six-month series of ranch and hunting sketches that ran from February through October. At the end of the run, *Century* published the book version *Ranch Life and the Hunting-Trail*. The reason for such a schedule of publication was a matter of money. Roosevelt joined other writers in a literary world that rewarded them for publishing short stories, chapters, narrative sketches, essays, and speeches first in magazines and then cobbling them together into books that earned money a second time. A clever writer — and certainly Roosevelt was one — could continue to refine, revise, and reorder pieces for use in other arenas, and in so doing build a respectable literary income. As the writer and social settlement founder Jane Addams put it, you make a book out of what you have on hand.

Roosevelt worked especially hard as a writer after stumbling as a politician in the fall of 1886. He was wooed into running for mayor against two men, Henry George, who was supported by organized labor, and former Democratic congressman Abram S. Hewitt, supported by Tammany Hall. The Republicans turned to Roosevelt in resistance, placing him in a contest impossible to win. As he put it to Lodge in a letter on October 20, 1886: "This must not be spoken outside; but in reality, not only is there not the slightest chance of my election, but there is at least an even chance of my suffering a very unusually heavy and damaging defeat."[30] The young politician was absolutely right, especially when Republican voters, fearing George's popularity, crossed over to vote for Hewitt, who won 90,552 votes to George's 68,110 and Roosevelt's 60,435.[31] The loss was not a story he wanted to talk about then or write about later.

It was at that moment the New York newspapers broke his "secret" engagement plans, and Roosevelt wrote to his cousin Laura Roosevelt, "Now, for something far more important than the mayoralty. Tomorrow I sail for Europe to marry Miss Edith Carow, and I wish your best wishes."[32] After the political trouncing, the eager young lover sailed for England on November 6, meeting onboard Cecil Arthur Spring-Rice, a British diplomat who would become an intimate friend, a sign of which was the fact that Roosevelt asked him to be best man at his wedding on December 2, 1886. From his honeymoon, he enthused to Anna, who had sent hairbrushes and a silver bottle as wedding gifts: "We had an idyllic three weeks trip; and it is extremely pleasant here in Florence. . . . I have plenty to do for I am hard at work on my Century articles."[33] Even in the throes of newly wedded bliss, the writer kept at his task.

The bride and groom took serious measure of their financial prospects. "My financial affairs for the past year make such a bad showing that Edith and I think very seriously of closing Sagamore Hill and going to the ranch for a year or two," he confided to Anna on January 3.[34] Things seemed dire enough that he had written his brother-in-law to sell his favorite horse, Sagamore, to pay back some of his debt to the Robinsons (the horse survived the sacrifice). But Theodore Roosevelt was not a man who suffered long. The damaging political defeat in New York and the scarcity of money, even for his honeymoon, seemed not to trouble him as he reveled in the successes of his year: "Meanwhile, at least 1886 has been as happy a year as any one could have."[35] Three days later, he wrote again to Anna, "You know, we *must* live; and so I do'n't much care whether I change my residence from New York or not."[36]

Three weeks later, he asked Corinne to send the address of his brother-in-law's shoe shop in London because he had been literally "racing up and down the neighboring hills, which I think will improve my health, which has not been benefited by rigorous sedentary seclusion and three weeks of daily overeating—but which is not good for shoe leather."[37] Restlessness spurred his literary life. Even on his honeymoon, he kept to his writing tasks, finishing all six sketches for *Century* while in Rome. On January 22, 1887, he reported to Corinne that Edith had "read them all over" and helped with the final edit; perhaps it was her hand that deftly struck out the offending "I"s. He acknowledged, "I don't know whether the Century will want them or not," and fretted over the publication date of the Benton book, wondering why it had not yet appeared. Both he, because he felt boxed in on his honeymoon, and Edith, because she feared spending so much money, decided to return to New York at the end of March. He confided, "I shall then go out west for a couple of weeks."[38] He signed the letter, "Your extravagant and irrelevant, but affectionate, brother."

With the completion of writing tasks that promised actual income, and the apology to his sister who, together with her husband, had sent him an additional 150 pounds, Theodore and Edith indulged in their last weeks alone in Italy. "Venice *is* perfectly lovely," he wrote to Corinne. "It is more strange than any other Italian town; and the architecture has a certain florid barbarism about it—Byzantine, dashed with something stronger—that appeals to some streak in my nature."[39] Florid barbarism suited his mood. The couple floated through the winding water streets in a gondola, knowing nothing yet about the chaotic blizzard that had again iced the Little Missouri River in Medora. The blizzard in the spring of 1886, as it turned out, had been a harbinger.

On November 7, 1886, and for a hundred days, snow and ice and bitter winds swept across the country from the Dakotas down through Kansas and Nebraska and into Texas, devastating ranches, families, and cattle in a sustained siege that buried people and animals, frozen under drifts of snow by unrelenting winds. Roosevelt's cattle, along with others across the plains, ran out of hay, so that by March when the thaws began, ranchers learned that only a third or even a fourth of most herds had survived.

Theodore and Edith returned to New York from Europe on March 28, 1887, and began to learn the details of their loss. He reported to Sewall, who had escaped from the blizzard along with Dow and their families, "About the only comfort I have out of it is that, at any rate, you and Wilmot are all right; I would not mind the loss of a few hundred if it was the only way to benefit you and Will—but it will be much more than that."[40] He visited Elkhorn to see for himself what had happened, and wrote Sewall about the losses that he and Sylvane Ferris discovered on the range, "You cannot imagine anything more dreary than the look of the Badlands. Everything was cropped as bare as a bone. The sagebrush was just fed out by the starving cattle. The snow lay so deep that nobody could get around; it was almost impossible to get a horse a mile." In every coulee, they found dead cattle, three hundred huddled together in one spot alone. His partner in the Maltese Cross herd, Bill Merrifield, claimed, "I don't know how many thousands we owned at Elkhorn and the Maltese Cross in the autumn of 1886, but after that terrible winter there wasn't a cow left, only a few hundred sick-looking steers."

"I am bluer than indigo about the cattle," Theodore wrote Anna on April 16, 1887; "it is even worse than I feared."[41] He had money on his mind, more clearly than ever before. "I wish I was sure I would lose no more than half the money ($80,000) I invested out here."[42] In a letter to Lodge, Roosevelt admitted the failure of ranch life. "Well, we have had a perfect smashup all through the cattle country of the northwest. The losses are crippling."[43] In characteristic fashion, he lamented the past and then turned his mind toward the future: "For the first time I have been utterly unable to enjoy a visit to my ranch. I shall be glad to get home."

He returned to New York City to earn his way with a pen, writing every day in the hope of bringing in $4,000 that year, augmenting the household income and mitigating the losses in Dakota.[44] *Thomas Hart Benton* came into print in 1887, followed in 1888 by three books in different genres: *Essays on Practical Politics*, two essays he had written as a New York assemblyman; *Gouverneur Morris*, a second biography in the American Statesmen series; and *Ranch Life and the Hunting-Trail*, the collection of essays from the *Century* series. On January 15, 1888, Roosevelt wrote to Jonas Van Duzer, a fellow New York legislator, "Like yourself, I shall probably never be in politics again." His ranch had not turned a profit, and he had new responsibilities as father to a son, Theodore "Teddy" Junior. He looked to his future as a writer: "My literary work occupies a good deal of my time; and I have on the whole done fairly well at it; I should like to write some book that would really rank as in the very first class, but I suppose this is a mere dream."[45]

In the fall of 1888, Roosevelt crafted his first piece of literary criticism, opining on Matthew Arnold's *Discourses on America*, the book he had found time to read after all. The British sage had just died, and the young American took issue with his charge that the new country lacked beauty, most especially in its literature: "Not even because of his [Arnold's] great authority would I be willing to miss from my bookshelves Irving and Hawthorne and Emerson and Cooper, Lowell, Longfellow, Whittier and Poe." He added the historians John Lothrop Motley and Francis Parkman. Because he was not a snob, Roosevelt included the Appalachian local-colorist Charles Egbert Craddock, who was actually Mary Noailles Murfree; the antebellum southern romantic Thomas Nelson Page; and the folklorist Joel Chandler Harris, creator of Uncle Remus. If literary America had not yet measured up, he retorted, it was because "taming a continent is nobler work than studying *belles lettres*."[46]

As he had chased desperadoes in the Dakotas and turned his pen to sketching rough American types, Roosevelt was creating a literary voice of his own. In the October issue of *Century* magazine, Walt Whitman's "Army Hospitals and Cases," a memoir of his nursing during the Civil War, was published alongside Roosevelt's "Frontier Types," the last chapter in *Ranch Life and the Hunting-Trail*.[47] As copies of the magazine arrived on both desks, the two New York storytellers began to take each other's measure.

"I like it: he gets pretty near the truth," Whitman confided to a friend. "He don't write it exactly as I would, of course: that's because he don't enter into it—puts on his glasses before he looks at it—writes it with a little the touch of a dude. Still, there is something alluring in the subject and the way it is handled: Roosevelt seems to have realized its character —its shape and size—to have honestly imbibed some of the spirit of that wild Western life." Roosevelt would later compare Whitman to Dante and hang a photograph of the poet in his office. But in 1888 the young writer had no way of knowing that Whitman admired his early promise as a writer, imbibing the spirit of the Wild West.

Chapter 5
"My Mistress Perforce"

No man, whatever may be his ability or industry,—even
if he be a ranchman,—can write history in its best form on
horseback. . . . Mr. Roosevelt, in making so good a work [*The
Winning of the West*], has clearly shown that he could make
a better one, if he would take more time in doing it.
{ William Frederick Poole, the *Atlantic*, 1889 }[1]

The strength of the work lies in the constant cropping out
[cropping up] of the author's own participation in the border
life of the present day. From his own experience, example after
example is drawn to illustrate situations that occurred in
Kentucky and Tennessee a hundred years before.
{ Stephen Weeks, American Academy of
Political and Social Science, 1895 }[2]

As *The Winning of the West* began taking shape, Roosevelt wrote to Francis Parkman, author of *The Oregon Trail: Sketches of Prairie and Rocky-Mountain Life* (1849), "I should like to dedicate this to you."[3] He sketched his book in a single sentence: "I am engaged on a work of which the first part treats of the extension to our frontier westward and southwestward during the twenty odd years from 1774 to 1796—the years of uninterrupted Indian warfare during which Kentucky and Tennessee were founded and grew to statehood, under such men as Daniel Boone and George Rogers Clark, John Sevier, James Robertson and Isaac Shelby." For a longer view, he pointed out that "the first chapter in the 'Benton' will give you an idea of the outline I intend to fill up." He would be interweaving literary genres, the writing he had done as a historian in *Thomas Hart Benton* and as a naturalist in *Ranch Life and the Hunting-Trail*. He quipped to Parkman, "Literature must be my mistress perforce, for though I really enjoy politics I appreciate perfectly the exceedingly short nature of my tenure."[4] The same qualms filled his letters to Henry Cabot Lodge. "I have made up my mind that I will go in especially for literature, simply taking the part in politics that a decent man should."[5] We hear notes of desire and anxiety.

The publisher George Haven Putnam recalled that Roosevelt was ambitious as a historian to do for the Southwest Territory what Parkman had done for the Northwest.[6] He admired the young writer's dramatic narratives, "vivid pictures which impressed themselves on the memory of the reader," and bragged that *The Winning of the West* was fashioned almost exclusively within the Putnam building on Twenty-Third Street in New York City, a short walk from Roosevelt's home. The book was printed and bound on the upper floors, written and revised on the second floor, and sold in the bookstore on the ground floor. All this could happen under a single roof because, after the publication of *The Naval War of 1812*, Roosevelt had entered the Putnam business as a silent partner. "Those who knew the man will realize the difficulty I might say the impracticality, of Roosevelt being 'silent' under any responsibilities," Putnam quipped. The secretary Mrs. Partington was heard to say that the young Roosevelt was "profligate in suggestions" about how best to run the business.

He had been gathering materials for *The Winning of the West* as far back as 1886 when he had written audaciously to Lyman Copeland Draper, an antiquarian who was hoarding a considerable collection of documents. In 1888 Roosevelt sent another request, clarifying what he especially wanted —"any material concerning Boone that you are not going to make use of— or anything about Crockett"—and vowing he did not intend to steal his thunder.[7] Draper never completed his book because, as he admitted, "I can write nothing so long as I fear there is a fact, no matter how small, as yet ungarnered."[8] The old man's fastidiousness rankled and amused Roosevelt, who had few such qualms as a scholar.

The young man worked, as he could, to gather a "mass of original matter in the shape of files of old newspapers, of unpublished letters, diaries, reports, and other manuscripts." He lived in a world where he had every opportunity to examine library documents at his leisure, even taking them home in the evenings.[9] His cryptic notes for the project survive as a series of fragments offering us glimpses into his thinking and writing.[10] Close to his heart are backwoodsmen who fought for the land west of the Alleghenies, men like Kasper Mansker, included in John Carr's *Early Times in Middle Tennessee*.[11] In the notebook, Roosevelt scribbles, "A Dutchman [German] who spoke broken English. Wonderful marksman; & woodsman. . . . Mansker said he had never seen such vast herds of buffalo at

French Lick (Nashville) covered whole face of county. . . . Made huts out of buffalo hides." In the book, he transforms Mansker into a character of his own: "The rude and fragmentary annals of the frontier are filled with the deeds of men, of whom Mansker can be taken as a type" (1:124). He comes to life under Roosevelt's pen: "When Mansker first went to the Bluffs, in 1769, the buffaloes were more numerous than he had ever seen them before; the ground literally shook under the gallop of the mighty herds, they crowded in dense throngs round the licks, and the forest re-sounded with their grunting bellows" (1:536). We feel and hear the im-mediacy of the passage: shaking ground, thudding hooves, and bellowing grunts. This is Roosevelt's writing at it best, melding scholarly history and visceral experience. We see him erasing the hundred years that sepa-rate him from his putative hero Mansker: "He and other woodsmen came back there off and on, hunting and trapping, and living in huts made of buffalo hides; just such huts as the hunters dwelt in on the Little Missouri and Powder rivers as late as 1883." As 1769 fades into 1883, Roosevelt crops up in the narrative, a literary device buttressed by several footnotes highlighting his own life along the Little Missouri in the 1880s.

Not surprisingly, Roosevelt imposes his own political ideas on Man-sker, a quintessential American-American: "A single generation, passed under the hard conditions of life in the wilderness, was enough to weld together into one people the representatives of these numerous and widely different races" (1:89). Backwoodsmen of Irish or German or Dutch or French descent, "whatever their blood, had become Americans, one in speech, thought, and character, clutching firmly the land." They shed Eu-rope like a bulky garment:

> They had lost all remembrance of Europe and all sympathy with things European; they had become as emphatically products native to the soil as were the tough and supple hickories out of which they fashioned the handles of the long, light axes. Their grim, harsh, nar-row lives were yet strangely fascinating and full of adventurous toil and danger; none but natures as strong, as freedom-loving, and as full of bold defiance as theirs could have endured existence on the terms which these men found pleasurable. Their iron surroundings made a mould which turned out all alike in the same shape . . . in dress, in customs, and in mode of life.

A backwoodsman himself, Theodore had bragged to Corinne, "I was pretty well done out with the work, the lack of sleep and the strain of the constant watchfulness, but I am as brown and as tough as a pine knot and feel equal to anything."[12]

"The Spread of the English-Speaking Peoples," his very first chapter, argues that language marks a people — not race or culture or history as much as language, the distinguishing feature of advanced civilization. "The English-speaking peoples now hold more and better land than any other American nationality or set of nationalities. They have in their veins less aboriginal American blood." Others have "tacitly allowed them to arrogate to themselves the title of 'Americans,' whereby to designate their distinctive and individual nationality" (1:30). To be clear, Roosevelt's English was American English; later, as president, he would work to simplify even its spelling.

The Winning of the West sketches the story of the European invasion of North America and the movement of so-called "civilized" people into what he (and other historians) considered the "wilderness" of the West in a long series of battles against what they believed were "savage" peoples living on the lands the Europeans ought to own. The colonizing wars among the Spanish, the French, and the British, especially the War of Independence, forge a new people, American-Americans, who are, for Roosevelt, exceptional and triumphal. The main hero of the early volumes is Daniel Boone, "a man of few words, cold and grave, accustomed to every kind of risk and hairbreadth escape, and as little apt to praise the deeds of others as he was to mention his own" (1:291). No western writer, including Owen Wister, ever said so much about masculine restraint in so few words.

Roosevelt paints on a large canvas, chronicling a Darwinian struggle for the future of the land. "Terrible deeds of prowess were done by the mighty men on either side. It was a war of stealth and cruelty, and ceaseless, sleepless watchfulness. The contestants had sinewy frames and iron wills, keen eyes and steady hands, hearts as bold as they were ruthless" (1:123). This was the very warrior that Theodore Roosevelt most admired, sinewy, iron-willed, keen, steady, and, when need be, ruthless. The Northwest, stretching far into the West, "founded not by individual Americans, but by the United States of America," is in truth "the heart of the nation" (2:200). His heartland belonged to European immigrants pushing westward. "The headwaters of the Missouri were absolutely unknown; nobody had penetrated the great plains, the vast seas of grass through which the Platte, the Little Missouri, and the Yellowstone ran. What lay beyond them, and between them and the Pacific, was not even guessed at"

(1:503). Readers in 1883 knew almost nothing about the Dakota Territories, much less about the lands beyond. He painted a West that had passed out of the hands of primitive tribes and through the stage of hunters and trappers in Kentucky and Tennessee and had arrived roughly on his doorstep at the Elkhorn Ranch.

For any writer, the hardest days come as a book makes its way into a reader's hands. On June 2, 1889, Roosevelt could tell Anna that the two volumes would be out in ten days, even as he doubted his skill: "It is wholly impossible for me to say if I have or have not properly expressed all the ideas that seethed vaguely in my soul as I wrote it."[13] He wrote to Lodge, complimenting him on his new book about George Washington: "It is no small triumph to have written such a book as that."[14] Roosevelt admitted, "You have now reached what I am struggling for; a *uniformly* excellent style." But by the end of the month, he could boast that the first edition of his book had nearly sold out.

On July 7, 1889, the *New York Times* reviewed *The Winning of the West* under the heading "Pushing Their Way."[15] The young writer could not have found a more fulsome audience. The anonymous voice in the review reminds us that Theodore Roosevelt was himself a New Yorker. The review bristles with clichés—"one man in a thousand" and "above the general run of men" who sheds "light on the subject." Casting a scornful eye on scholars, the reviewer cautions, "In some minor respects there will be some who may differ from Mr. Roosevelt, but this may be asserted, that it will be difficult to conceive how anybody can ever come better prepared, in a personal sense, for this precise kind of work than the author." He chides sedentary scholars: "It is not within our province to expatiate on the literary qualities of historians who in their closets seek for highly-clever second-hand inspirations." Such a pedant may journey to Watauga Creek to see for himself an old beech tree with carvings, but he could never decipher a line like "D. Boon cilled a bar on tree in the year 1760," as Roosevelt, a "ranchman of to-day," could easily do. He even attaches a letter from John Allison verifying the carving: "The tree is a beech, still standing, though fast decaying."

The reviewer, shallow and adoring, caught Roosevelt cropping himself into the purported history and thought what he was doing made sense, because his defining credential was not his birthplace, 28 East Twentieth Street, New York City, but his Elkhorn Ranch on the Little Missouri River in the Dakotas. The reviewer was convinced that Roosevelt could tell the story of the pioneering spirit because he shared "the living bond of human sympathy" with backwoodsmen, hunters, ranchers, and cowboys. He praised the prose style and quoted Roosevelt liberally:

> "A grim, stern people, strong and simple, powerful for good and evil, swayed by gusts of stormy passion, the love of freedom rooted in their very hearts' core. Their lives were harsh and narrow; they gained their bread by their blood and sweat in the unending struggle with the wild ruggedness of nature. They suffered terrible injuries at the hands of the red men, and on their foes they waged a terrible warfare in return. They were relentless, revengeful, suspicious, knowing neither ruth nor pity; they were also upright, resolute, and fearless, loyal to their friends, and devoted to their country. In spite of their many failings, they were of all men the best fitted to conquer the wilderness and hold it against their enemies."

Roosevelt had created out of fairly plain language a myth of the West that put an Old New Yorker in the saddle. What could be better than that? His hometown newspaper declared his writing "true literary art."

Historians were not as willing to give Roosevelt a pass in the intellectual arena, where they eyed his work with suspicion. In November, William Frederick Poole, head of the newly established Newberry Library and president of the American Historical Association and the American Library Association, was asked by William Dean Howells to review *The Winning of the West* for the *Atlantic Monthly*.[16] Poole, who wrote anonymously, applauded Roosevelt's entry into a scholarly field filled with "thin and sensational" tales of "doubtful authenticity." He thought the young man, familiar with colloquial language, brought to the field a literary style that was "natural, simple, and picturesque, without any attempt at fine writing." Poole especially favored the use of primary materials: "Few writers of American history have covered a wider or better field of research, or are more in sympathy with the best modern method of studying history from original sources." Roosevelt held promise as a writer and a scholar. The praise ended there.

"No man, whatever may be his ability or industry, — even if he be a ranchman, — can write history in its best form on horseback," Poole mocked, drawing one of the first caricatures of Theodore Roosevelt. The bumptious writer "tripped on level ground where there is no need of it." The book was riddled with errors because the writer was too eager to be done: "We have a feeling that he might profitably have spent more time in consulting and collating the rich materials to which he had access."

He had raced through the Haldimand Collection in Ottawa or skipped over portions of the Michigan Pioneer Collection, missing "a mine of information which has never been used in any Western history." Poole hit hard: "Mr. Roosevelt, in making so good a work, has clearly shown that he could make a better one, if he would take more time in doing it."[17] He took the author to task for one error after another, painstakingly detailing what Roosevelt had misread or failed to read. He scolded him for disparaging the work of his elders: "Writers, and young writers especially, — Mr. Roosevelt is only thirty-one years of age, — are apt, in the glow of composition, to deal in sharp epithets and sneering comments concerning preceding writers who they think have erred; and these passages are commonly toned down, or, what is better, canceled, in a deliberate revision of the manuscript." As he held the book in his hands, Poole thought the sneers looked peevish on the printed page.

On October 27, with the November review already in his hands, Roosevelt shot off a letter to the *Atlantic Monthly*. "I do not know whether it is usual for an author to write to a reviewer; but yours is the first criticism of my book from which I have learnt anything," he disarmed his critic.[18] Stinging from the charge of hastiness, he defended his use of time: the rigors of his political duties had compromised the book he was writing. "I either had to get it out at once or wait several years; I ought to have done the latter, I suppose, — but I didn't." The voice is fresh, eager, alert, and combative. Cheekily reviewing the review, Roosevelt took Poole's measure: "It was a real (albeit not unmixed) pleasure to me to see it; for curiously enough I have never so far met a man with whom I could discuss this early western history, or who knew anything about it as a whole, and yours was the first article I read on the subject which I felt was written with knowledge and authority." A pedant's pen, however, was not what Roosevelt was reaching for: "What I am especially aiming at in my history is to present the important facts, and yet to avoid being drowned in a mass of detail." He favored haste in composition over "intolerable antiquarian minuteness," with Draper perhaps most in his mind. Even as the *Atlantic* issue was arriving on newsstands, Poole was responding to his young colleague: "It is very gratifying to me to have you say that you 'felt that the article was written by a man who knew the subject' and that you had 'learned something from it.'" It turned out Poole had an ego, too. He was won over.

In December, the two men met at the closing session of the American Historical Association's annual meeting. From the minutes, we know that the U.S. Civil Service commissioner Theodore Roosevelt gave an extemporaneous address, "Certain Phases of the Westward Movement during the Revolutionary War," that was taken down by the secretary. We recognize his voice, confident and clear: "The foundation of this great Federal Republic was laid by backwoodsmen, who conquered and held the land west of the Alleghanies, and thus prepared the way for the continental dominion of the English race in America."[19] A lively discussion ensued. In his own term as president of the American Historical Association in 1912, Roosevelt would call for "History as Literature," the very blending of historical and imaginative storytelling he was crafting in the late nineteenth century.

Getting from the first two volumes to the third took him five years, not because he toed the mark as a scholar, reading more deeply in archives to enrich the story, but because he turned his pen to other projects, keeping in mind the money he could earn as a writer. Over these same years, Roosevelt wrote a brief biography of the founding father Gouverneur Morris, in the American Statesman series.[20] His Benton volume had not gone particularly well, and he confessed to Lodge, "Do you know, I can not help thinking John Jay more deserving to have a place in the Statesmen series than Morris, though the last is so much more amusing."[21] In the book, he characterized Morris as able, fearless, cultivated, devoted, tough, having as his most desirable distinction "affection for things American." Not much to build a story on.

From the Ryan Hotel in Saint Paul, Minnesota, on October 1, 1888, Roosevelt had responded to a book offer from Brander Matthews, the literary adviser at Longmans, Green, and Company, to write a history of New York City for the American Historic Towns series (Lodge was writing the volume on Boston).[22] "I should like much to do the work; and will undertake it with pleasure if a little lee way is allowed me to finish up some matters which I *must* get through first," Roosevelt promised, even as he plunged into the 1888 presidential election, campaigning for Republican Benjamin Harrison over Democrat Grover Cleveland.[23] For his work, President Harrison appointed Roosevelt to the United States Civil Service Commission, a job he would hold over the next six years—into President Cleveland's administration—as he argued strongly for reform of the patronage system, insisting that government jobs ought to be based on merit alone and not party affiliation. Even with the contract signed, Roosevelt pushed the deadline back on the New York history: "I am going to spend six weeks after the 5th of August out West among the bears and cowboys, as I think I have fairly earned a holiday."[24] Each year, he saved weeks in late summer for hunting trips in the West; nothing got in the way of that.

From his Civil Service office in Washington, D.C., as time allowed, he wrote *New York*, publishing the volume in January 1891. In his preface, he declares himself not a scholar but a casual observer of "the workings of the town's life, social, commercial, and political, at successive periods with their sharp transformations and contrasts," and he meant "to trace the causes which gradually changed a little Dutch trading hamlet into a huge American city."[25] We note his verbs: "sketch," "trace," "outline," and even his "barely touching." The book, unimaginative and perfunctory, traces themes he was working out in other histories. For example, we recognize his call for Americans without prefix, not Irish-Americans, nor German or even Native-Americans, if anything American-Americans. Over two hundred pages, he gave his readers information that many no doubt already knew, and the book was a dud. In the literary business, and he referred to himself in a letter to Matthews as a "literary feller," one writer often helps another, each building his own career. Thus it was Brander Matthews who, without signing his name, wrote a most admiring review of *New York* in *Century Magazine*.[26]

The lure of nature writing was always strong in Roosevelt, and during the lull between volumes of *The Winning of the West*, he relaxed into writing *The Wilderness Hunter* (1893). Two poetic epigraphs invite readers into his narrative, the first from "The Ship in the Desert" by Joaquin Miller, the "Poet of the Sierras," in a passage that places lumbermen, who had climbed the "rock-built breasts of earth" and seen "the face of God," back in camp where "They saw the silences / Move by and beckon." The second lines are from Walt Whitman's *Leaves of Grass* in a passage that welcomes us to join lumbermen in their winter camp: "The blazing fire at night, the sweet taste of supper, the talk, the bed of / hemlock boughs, and the bear-skin." The lines remind us that Roosevelt was a reader, an admirer of language that evokes mood, as he wrote, "The free, self-reliant, adventurous life, with its rugged and stalwart democracy; the wild surroundings, the grand beauty of the scenery, the chance to study the ways and habits of the woodland creatures — all these unite to give the career of the wilderness hunter its peculiar charm."[27]

Daniel Boone appears as the archetype of the American backwoods hunter, who heralded the arrival of the pioneer who, in turn, conquered the wilderness by wresting the land from the supposed "savages"; and thus, step by bloody step, "often leap by leap, the frontier of settlement was pushed westward" (15). The book traces familiar ground without the intrusion of footnotes, and the reader of *The Wilderness Hunter* arrives fairly quickly in the West that Roosevelt knew firsthand, a West devoid of buffalo herds and beaver-laden streams, especially after the blizzard of 1887. The lack of big game, small game, even songbirds, may well have caused him to consider ways to ameliorate the damage done by unwise and unplanned over-ranching, and heedless profiteering by brutal commercial game hunters.

How could he bring his two "mistresses," literature and politics, together? Inviting a dozen or so friends, all of them interested in large-animal hunting, and all men of means, to Anna's Fifth Avenue apartment, Theodore proposed an association, dubbed the Boone and Crockett Club, to promote game laws, good hunting ethics, and governmental policies to foster game preserves and seasonal regulations. By 1888, it had been legally established, with by-laws, policy aims, and Theodore Roosevelt as president. His literary critic and now friend George Bird Grinnell was second in command, and together they began planning a series of publications by the club, to be edited by the two of them, and for which they would both write. Roosevelt remained president until 1894, and by that time, the organization's power and farsightedness were obvious. Yellowstone National Park was rescued from desolation by commercial enterprises; plans were afoot for the formation of the Bronx Zoo; sequoia groves were protected in California; and Boone and Crockett books were well under way: *American Big-Game Hunting* (1893), *Hunting in Many Lands* (1895), and *Trail and Camp-Fire* (1897). Over the years, with Roosevelt looking on, the group inspired the American Bison Foundation, which almost single-handedly kept the American bison a viable species in the American West, and such groups as Ducks Unlimited and Trout Unlimited, as well as offering lobbying and financial support to encourage the formation of national forests, new national parks, and a long series of national wildlife refuges. Conservation and wildlife preservation without the Boone and Crockett Club would look much different from how it does today.

Roosevelt used political activism to further his writing career, and the Boone and Crockett books remain to this day editions of scientific and hunting literature in late nineteenth-century America that are not only beautifully produced and edited, but in every way reputable. Roosevelt—the writer, the wildlife biologist, the politician—enhances America's ability to conserve precious natural resources. Did he come up with the idea for the Boone and Crockett Club by himself? Did he pattern it after his uncle Robert Roosevelt's ground-breaking work to preserve game and commercial fishing in the Hudson River? Did he found this service organization to pay homage to his late father? It scarcely matters. Having founded the club, and driven it, and protected it, he could also use it to further his standing as a nature writer, a science writer, and visionary of conservation and preservation of the natural world. Not bad for the myopic boy who in Oyster Bay used to listen to birdsong because he could not see the singing birds.

By 1894, back at his task of *The Winning of the West*, Roosevelt wrote to the emerging scholar Frederick Jackson Turner, professor of American history at the University of Wisconsin, who had brought new life to the American Historical Association in July of 1893 with his essay "The Significance of the Frontier in American History." Roosevelt told Turner that he intended to use and cite his ideas in the third volume of *The Winning of the West*. "I think you have struck some first class ideas, and have put into definite shape a good deal of thought which has been floating around rather loosely."[28] Certainly, it had floated rather loosely in Roosevelt's mind and in the writing he had been doing for a decade.

The Harvard Collection includes a handwritten draft of the third volume of *The Winning of the West* that offers a window onto Roosevelt's writing method at this stage of his career. The manuscript is legible, and we see him in high compositional mode, purifying the prose, making the writing clearer, always more readable, bringing emphasis to ideas that he wanted to highlight, leading toward stronger and more coherent individual sentences. One assumes he is writing as he goes, perhaps from cryptic notes, and the assurance of the hand suggests, as Putnam described it, that the young historian penned the first draft as a nearly finished draft. If so, the writing reveals Theodore Roosevelt's uncanny talent for designing a story in his head, nimbly sorting and synthesizing vast stores of detail, before putting pen to paper and then moving quickly down the page in a steady cursive hand.

The manuscript chapter, "The Northwest Territory; Ohio, 1787–1790," reads well even without its inserted revisions. Changes in the prose are relatively rare for a writer little given to reworking passages or altering the basic shape of his narrative. The pen moved to strengthen a verb or noun or subtract an adjective, showing signs of a mind focused on precision. It struck out the adjective "hard" and moved the adverb "directly" and alternated "first" and "early" to strengthen the opening lines, but most of the draft stands untouched:

So far the work of the backwoodsman in exploring, conquering, and holding the West had been work undertaken solely on individual initiative. The nation as a whole had not directly shared in it. The frontiersmen who chopped the first trails across the Alleghanies, who earliest wandered through the lonely Western lands, and who first built stockade hamlets on the banks of the Watauga, the Kentucky, and the Cumberland, acted each in consequence of his own restless eagerness for adventure and possible gain.

Roosevelt's revising process was largely one of accretion. Rethinking, for him, almost always meant adding sentences, even paragraphs; you can see how he wedged new language between the lines, or, turning the page, how he placed new text in balloons in such tiny letters that the typesetter must have strained to grasp the words.

After reading the third volume of *The Winning of the West*, Turner wrote an anonymous review in the *Nation*, taking the strident historian to task.[29] Roosevelt fired back to the editors for the reviewer's identity. He then wrote a letter to Turner in his typically sly way: "It was a great pleasure to me to find that you were my reviewer" because it was "intelligent criticism."[30] We hear the catty tone: "I hope you will write a serious work on the subject. I know of no one so well qualified for the task." Turner, who had been raised in what we call today the upper Midwest (then the western frontier), believed in the power of frontier community. The West, as he could see from the world around him, was won by the steady building of local and county governments, the building blocks of democracy. He complained that Roosevelt failed to acknowledge the contributions of local, agrarian efforts in shaping the West, and Roosevelt retorted, "My aim is especially to show who the frontiersmen were and what they did, as they gradually conquered the West." As for the charge that he had paid scant attention to the documents of land companies, he asserted, "The real importance of the movement came in the settlers themselves, whose habits of thought, modes of life, and systems of government left their mark stamped deep on the ground; while the traces left by the land companies were comparatively few." From his experience as a bureaucrat — and he was the one with practical experience — the documents of committees and companies could not be trusted to tell a straight story. Any one of us who ever put together a committee report might agree.

Turner saw an American West won by yeoman farmers, artisans, and entrepreneurs, a collective that established the agrarian republic, the regeneration of society, argues Richard Slotkin in *Gunfighter Nation: The Myth of the Frontier in Twentieth-Century America*.[31] Turner was at heart a populist, in stark contrast to the progressive Roosevelt. In the American West, Roosevelt saw an evolutionary struggle among racial groups, where indigenous peoples were defeated by backwoodsmen—"archetypes of freedom"—who in turn were replaced by cowboys and ranchers, much like himself. Slotkin hits upon Roosevelt's tendency to crop up in the story, so much so that he "makes his own history the fulfillment of the larger historical processes he had invoked." In *The Winning of the West*, the arc of history bends toward the Little Missouri, clearing the path for the owner of the Elkhorn Ranch.

All writing is, to some extent, autobiographical, the writer often hidden behind the scene, offstage, out of direct action, but Theodore Roosevelt found ways, consciously and unconsciously, to bring himself onto the stage, as he would do most openly in *The Rough Riders*.

Biographers refer to the sharp exchange between the rival historians by quoting the end of Roosevelt's letter to Turner: "I am a very busy man, and it is awfully difficult for me to get away." To complete future volumes would require even more time: "I certainly can't until I get entirely out of political life; a move I am strongly tempted to make." With Turner's criticisms still in his mind, Roosevelt wrote again on April 26, 1895. "I don't think after all that our views as to the fundamental unity of the Westerners differ widely," he soothed his colleague, adding that he was using Turner's ideas at that very moment in "a chapter I am writing."[32] He was a good politician, no matter what hand he had to play.

The truth is that Theodore Roosevelt's life was a whirlwind during the last decade of the nineteenth century, as his mind moved from idea to idea with a speed hard to imagine for a sedentary scholar like Turner who lived in a world of books and classrooms. The month he claimed to be stepping away from political life, Roosevelt was in fact looking for his next political job, not surprisingly preferring a seat on the New York Police Commission to a seat on Street Cleaning. On April 14, 1895, in a letter to Anna, he explained, "I would like to do my share in governing the city after our great victory; and so far as may be I would like once more to have my voice in political matters."[33] Roosevelt took the job of police commissioner in May 1895. He wrote to Indiana lawyer Lucius Burrie Swift, editor of the *Civil Service Chronicle*, about the dismal chances for reform in New York City. "There are certain evils which I fear cannot possibly be suppressed in a city like New York in our present stage of existence," he offered as

THEODORE ROOSEVELT

a pragmatic reading of social evolution.[34] "I shall do my best to find out how to minimize them and make them least offensive, but more than this I fear cannot be done," he soberly pledged.

He sold an essay, "Six Years of Civil Service Reform," to *Scribner's Magazine* in June of 1895 for $175, and a review of Benjamin Kidd's *Social Evolution* to *North American Review*, where he argued against Kidd's notion that the fittest populations are forged by the keenest pressure. "The generals and admirals, the poets, philosophers, historians and musicians, the statesmen and judges, the law-makers and law-givers, the men of arts and of letters, the great captains of war and of industry — all these come from the classes where the struggle for the bare means of subsistence is least severe, and where the rate of increase is relatively smaller than in the classes below."[35] Roosevelt was working on a theory of social evolution, based on eugenics, that would lead him later to lecture prosperous white women on the optimal number (five or even six) of children to have in order to secure the best chances for social progress, to produce generals and poets and philosophers and historians and musicians and statesmen. We look closely at his list as a measure of what he valued and in what order. He was a statesman and historian, not a general or admiral, not yet a colonel. Certainly he would never be a poet.

Sitting restlessly in an office, riding his bicycle to work for his only exercise, the young commissioner began exploring the city he was entrusted to protect. He wrote Anna on June 8, 1895, about a "night I passed in tramping the streets, finding out by personal inspection how the police were doing their duty."[36] The next morning, lining up the group of frightened cops, he reprimanded or fined them for neglecting their duties. The next week, he enthused, "Twice I have spent the night in patrolling New York on my own account, to see exactly what the men were doing."[37] He bragged of going forty hours without sleep and being in robust health: "But in spite of my work I really doubt whether I have often been in better health." Even in New York City he could become tough as a "hickory nut." His police work was practical, without a touch of the academic, and absorbed his energy and imagination.

"I have not tried to write a line of my book since I took the office," he crowed to Anna. And the next week, he continued, "I am immensely amused and interested in my work. It keeps me so busy I can hardly think."[38] He was thinking, but in a new way, about a wider world than Harvard or Dakota had offered. "These midnight rambles are great fun. My whole work brings me in contact with every class of people in New

York, as no other work possibly could; and I get a glimpse of the real life of the swarming millions. Finally, I do really feel that I am accomplishing a good deal." He reveled in an active life that left little time for writing, a pleasure any procrastinating writer can taste.

Writing to Lodge on July 20, 1895, he joked about his summer with groveling politicians of the baser sort.[39] "Two or three nights a week I have to stay in town; Sunday I spend in the country; the other days I ride to and from the station on my bicycle, leaving my house at half past seven in the morning, spending a perfect whirl of eight hours in New York, and returning just in time for a short play with the children before I get dressed for supper." The political fights were savage, and the press hounded him: "The *World, Herald, Sun, Journal* and *Advertiser* are shrieking with rage; the *Staats-Zeitung* is fairly epileptic; the *Press* stands by me nobly. The *Tribune* and the *Times* more tepidly; the *Evening Post* has been afraid of its life, and has taken refuge in editorials that are so colorless as to be comical." The swirl of language gave him an adrenaline rush. "I don't care a snap of my finger," he swaggered; "I am going to fight no matter what the opposition is."

When he later wrote in his autobiography about this period, he defined a literary credo that was only just coming into his mind as the nineteenth century turned to the twentieth: "I have always had a horror of words that are not translated into deeds, of speech that does not result in action — in other words, I believe in realizable ideals and in realizing them, in preaching what can be practiced and then in practicing it."[40] The man of action was thinking of ways to put language to work.

His mentor was the Danish immigrant writer Jacob Riis, whose best-seller *How the Other Half Lives: Studies among the Tenements of New York* appeared first as a series in *Scribner's Magazine* in 1889 and then as a book in 1890. Riis pointed the way for writers to use the language of law to bring about social change. On December 4, 1894, Roosevelt wrote a letter to Riis about Mayor-elect Strong: "From you I feel he could get information such as he could not get from anyone else about the condition of our schools and about what can be done. . . . I know hardly anyone who has done more than you have to give people an intelligent appreciation of the great social problems of the day and who has approached these problems with more common sense and sobriety."[41] Common sense and sobriety were always close to Roosevelt's heart, and, over the years, Riis stayed in his mind. When he left New York to go to the Department of the Navy, he wrote, "For these last two years you have been my main prop and comfort."[42] In 1903, Riis would craft a biographical mash-note of sorts in *Theodore Roosevelt: The Citizen*, singing the praises of the president as Roosevelt began campaigning for his first actual election to the highest office.[43] And in his autobiography, Roosevelt would remember "Jacob Riis had drawn an indictment of the things that were wrong, pitifully and dreadfully wrong, with the tenement homes and the tenement lives of our wage-workers."[44] It would be the job of government to answer that indictment with the language of law.

As Roosevelt considered how the other half lived in New York City in the 1890s, a period of financial depression throughout the country, he read the work of the young radical fiction writers of his day, all of them followers of the French novelist and theorist Émile Zola, whose *Le roman expérimental* urged them to turn their imaginations to social conditions of the working class. Zola called his theory "literary naturalism." In a letter to Brander Matthews on December 7, 1894, Roosevelt considered such naturalistic tendencies in the fiction of Hamlin Garland, who called his own literary theory "veritism." Garland published "Only a Lumber Jack" in *Harper's Weekly* that month, and Roosevelt thought it a good story, not as morbid as Garland's other work, but he had a considerable caveat: "It looks to me as though he were going to, in a somewhat different way, suffer as Howells has done, by taking a jaundiced view of life."[45] William Dean Howells, editor of the *Atlantic Monthly* and arbiter of American realism, had put his pen into the service of social reform, a literary movement that irritated Roosevelt as a politician and more so as a reader. It is a battle he would wage all his life with Howells and Garland as well as with Zola, Thomas Hardy, Stephen Crane, Frank Norris, and Theodore Dreiser.

Most writers depicted the plight of the poor without having had visceral encounters with poverty itself. "I am amused at one thing," Roosevelt told Matthews: Garland's absurd use of "greasy quilts" to signify discomfort and unhappiness. From his own experiences in the West, Roosevelt begged to differ. "Well, they are distressing to an overcivilized man; but for my own pleasure this year when I was out on the antelope plains I got into a country where I didn't take my clothes off for ten days," he roared. Greasy quilts offered a sense of holiday from the sort of respectable cleanliness Garland valued in Boston. But Roosevelt pulled back slightly from making full heroes of western men: "The life as a whole is a decidedly healthy and attractive one to men who do not feel the need of mental recreation and stimulus — and few of them do."[46] As for Garland, he would do well to write stories and not literary philosophy, "where the propriety of his purpose is marred by the utter crudity of his half-baked ideas," like those of the "veritists."

On August 6, Roosevelt wrote to the *Atlantic Monthly* editor Horace Elisha Scudder, recommending that he publish an article by the *Evening Post* reporter Joseph Lincoln Steffens about the police department. "He is a personal friend of mine; and he has seen all of our work at close quarters. He and Mr. Jacob Riis have been the two members of the Press who have most intimately seen almost all that went on here."[47] Later, in his autobiography, Steffens would recall the three of them: "It was all breathless and sudden, but Riis and I were soon describing the situation to him. . . . It was just as if we three were the police board, T.R., Riis, and I, and as we got T.R. calmed down we made him promise to go a bit slow, to consult with his colleagues also."[48] Even as TR spent the week at Harvard for his fifteenth reunion among his Porcellian friends, he began police work on what he called "an ugly snag": "I am working as I never worked before."[49] The Sunday Excise Law banished alcohol sales on the Christian Sabbath, and Roosevelt, never a drinker himself, determined that the law would be followed, even though he thought it too strict.[50] A year of work as police commissioner wore on him, and he joked to Anna that the "screeching mendacity" of the *Herald* and the *World* had worn thin, and that his political successes were "gradually growing evident even to the dull public mind."[51]

Astonishingly, in this year of sweat as a public servant, Roosevelt finished the proofs on the next volume of *The Winning of the West*. "I shall be through the hardest part of my work both literary and official; I shall then have finished a year of as hard work and of as much worry and responsibility as a man could well have." He could not know, of course, that harder days were not far ahead, but the truth is that what Theodore Roosevelt most feared was a life with nothing to do.

Volume four of *The Winning of the West* was published in 1896, and an urbane review soon followed written by Stephen Beauregard Weeks, who had earned the first PhD in English from the University of North Carolina and then another in history from Johns Hopkins University. Writing for the *Annals of the American Academy of Political and Social Science*, he neatly summed up Roosevelt's long project "to tell the story of the invasion and taming of the western wilderness, the driving back of the Indian possessors, and the erection of free governments on the soil thus wrested at great expense of blood and treasure from the hands of the savage."[52]

Crediting Roosevelt with using the Draper manuscripts (after Draper's death) and attending more to his scholarly task than he had in the first two volumes, he admired the colorful stories and seemed amused by diatribes against other historians.

Weeks trained a scholarly eye on what the *New York Times* reviewer had hinted at: "The strength of the work lies in the constant cropping out of the author's own participation in the border life of the present day." Theodore Roosevelt felt utterly comfortable insinuating himself into the history he was telling. "From his own experience, example after example is drawn to illustrate situations that occurred in Kentucky and Tennessee a hundred years before," Weeks noted. Roosevelt drew from his life in the Dakotas especially in his portrayal of the clash between Anglo-Saxons and Indians, where he wrote: "'It is idle to dispute about the rights or wrongs of the contest. Two peoples, in two stages of culture which were separated by untold ages, stood face to face; one or the other had to perish: and the whites went forward from sheer necessity.'" Weeks observed, "There is no mistaking the tone of these sentences." As for differences between the North and the South, Weeks put it simply: "The land to the north of Ohio represents the spirit of collectivism; the land to the south the spirit of individualism." He understood the battle between Turner, who argued for the collective, and Roosevelt, who championed the individual.

Reviewing the same volume of *The Winning of the West* for the American Historical Association, Frederick Jackson Turner began in praise of Roosevelt: "He has rescued a whole movement in American development from the hands of unskillful annalists."[53] The work was innovative because the author pushed against the prejudices of established scholars who had relied on received knowledge: "He has made use of widely scattered original sources, not heretofore exploited." Roosevelt's prose moved with "graphic vigor," and his mind ranged beyond local history into considerations of the wider world, especially involvements with France and Spain. Turner agreed with other reviewers that Roosevelt worked from firsthand experience in the American West and thus wrote with an integrity not earned by other eastern scholars. He admired the author's sympathy with frontiersmen and agreed, for the most part, with his "courageous and virile" ways of depicting "Indian relations" in what he called "the wastes of the continent." Turner, that is to say, shared Roosevelt's prejudices. He saw verve in the narrative style ("It is the dramatic and picturesque aspects of the period that most interest him—the Indian fighting, the intrigues with Spain and the exploration of the far West"), a style at times without equal ("The campaigns of St. Clair and Wayne are not likely to be better presented than in the author's pages").

Turner's hesitations were the same ones he had had with the previous volumes. The writing comes with "dash and lightness of touch" at the price of scholarly veracity: "He frequently fails to work his subject out into its less obvious relations; and the marks of actual haste are plain in careless proof-reading and citations." At the heart of the story, Turner pointed to intrigues and conspiracies in the conquests of western territories, including those of Aaron Burr, Colonel Morgan, Elijah Clark, and especially George Rogers Clark. "Mr. Roosevelt's account of George Rogers Clark's relations to Genet in an effort to lead an expedition against the Spaniards at New Orleans, is of much value." It is here that we see why the Draper materials were pivotal to the work Roosevelt was doing. "This part of Clark's career has been ignored or glossed over by his admirers, but on the basis of the Draper Manuscripts, in the State Historical Society of Wisconsin, Mr. Roosevelt elucidates the interesting episode." Turner's main charge against Roosevelt — a considerable one for a historian basing his argument on the validity of his original sources — was that he simply had failed to work thoroughly. "If Mr. Roosevelt had given more painstaking attention . . . he might perhaps have secured important documents. . . . There is no evidence that he attempted to do this."

Turner, however, heard a new note in Theodore Roosevelt's prose: *haec fabula docet* — using narrative to preach a moral lesson. "He does not hesitate to use his pages as a means of impressing his views of parties and party policies upon his readers." Turner caught Roosevelt, the politician, in the act of riding a hobbyhorse of his own, military preparedness, and quoted the insistent voice: "'These facts may, with advantage, be pondered by those men of the present day who are either so ignorant or of such lukewarm patriotism that they do not wish to see the United States keep prepared for war.'" His story of how the West was won, that is to say, veered into a didactic rant, much like the one in his *Naval War of 1812*, on the wisdom and necessity of preparedness for war on land and most especially on water. "While one can appreciate the energetic Americanism of Mr. Roosevelt," Turner scoffed, "one can also lament that he finds it necessary to use his history as the text for a sermon to a stiff-necked generation." The historian had morphed into the politician.

Roosevelt shot back with a compliment, a whine, and then a volley. "You are a master of the subject, and therefore you can write the only kind of review I care to read."[54] He used the excuse of time: "I have been worked very hard indeed for the last eight years, and it was a physical impossibility to neglect my duties as Civil Service Commissioner or a Police Commissioner, so I either had to stop historical work entirely, or do just as I have done." Then he grew feisty. He meant to sketch a narrative for a general reader, and for that task saw no reason to "again thrash out the straw" of scholarly debates. Academic minutiae may not yield truth and may blind one to the truth, he sneered. Turner had dismissed his chapters on the Louisiana Purchase and Aaron Burr's conspiracy: "They add nothing of importance to the work of Henry Adams." That line set Roosevelt off: "I must have failed to make clear my effort to accentuate the most important point in the whole affair, and the very point which Henry Adams failed to see, namely that the diplomatic discussion to which he devotes so much space, though extremely interesting, and indeed very important as determining the method of the transfer, did not at all determine the fact that the transfer had to be made. It was the growth of the Western settlements that determined this fact." Pedants like Henry Adams and Turner might thresh out the straw but never find the grain. He ended the letter abruptly—"There!"—and with a lie, "I have not written another critic of my work, but with you it is interesting to enter into a discussion."

Turner agreed with Poole and establishment historians that Roosevelt simply could not stay on task: "But the special student must regret that Mr. Roosevelt does not find it possible to regard history as a more jealous mistress, and to give more time, greater thoroughness of investigation, particularly in foreign archives, and more sobriety of judgment to his work" (176).

Roosevelt was working for money in the 1890s and not earning as much as he hoped for. Writing to his friend Frederic Remington, whose first one-man show in 1890 made him a commercial success, he joked, "I ever so wished to be a millionaire or indeed any person other than a literary man with a large family of small children and a taste for practical politics and bear hunting, as when you have pictures to sell."[55] And then he added in admiration and envy: "It seems to me that you in your line, and Wister is his, are doing the best work in America today." The young historian knew that he was not yet doing his best work and in truth did not yet know what his best line would be.

Chapter 6
Words into Blows

"'Tis 'Th' Biography iv a Hero be Wan who Knows.' 'Tis
'Th' Darin' Exploits iv a Brave Man be an Actual Eye Witness.'
'Tis 'Th' Account iv th' Desthruction iv Spanish Power in th' Ant
Hills,' as it fell fr'm th' lips iv Tiddy Rosenfelt an' was took down be
his own hands. . . . If his valliant deeds didn't get into this book 'twud
be a long time befure they appeared in Shafter's histhry iv th' war.
No man that bears a gredge again' himsilf 'll iver be governor iv
a state. An' if Tiddy done it all he ought to say so an' relieve th'
suspinse. But if I was him I'd call th' book 'Alone in Cubia.'"
{ Finley Peter Dunne, "A Book Review," 1900 }[1]

Theodore Roosevelt sought ways of moving words into deeds, language into force. He had used words to tell the story of naval prowess in *The Naval War of 1812* and then used four volumes of words to tell the heroic stories of *The Winning of the West*. What he discovered in 1898 was a way to move words into deeds as he led a military regiment into the Spanish-American War, and then to move deeds back into words as he told the story of his own exploits in *The Rough Riders*, a book we might think of as the last volume in his long history of how the West was won. "I always hate words unless they mean blows," he thundered what we might call the Roosevelt literary doctrine in a letter to Anna on March 30, 1896.[2] He would repeat the doctrine in his autobiography as he admonished his male readers about military service: "When a man takes such a position, he ought to be willing to make his words good by his deeds unless there is some very strong reason to the contrary. He should pay with his body."[3] Cuba offered Roosevelt his chance at something, to be a soldier, in the saddle, on horseback, in charge of rough-riding desperadoes, the strenuous life he craved, his first real chance to be a man.

For years, Theodore Roosevelt had been spoiling for a fight, one where he could become a soldier, a mark of manhood that had eluded his father, who had, along with other Old New Yorkers, hired someone to take his place in the Civil War. In the summer of 1886, the United States and Mexico had nearly come to blows over the death of Captain Emmet Crawford in a border incident, and Theodore "*qua* cowboy, not *qua* statesman," had confided to Henry Cabot Lodge how disappointed he was that Secretary of State Thomas Francis Bayard had negotiated the dispute. "If a war had come off I would surely have had behind me as utterly reckless a set of desperados, as ever sat in the saddle."[4] He meant, even then, to raise a regiment of what he called "rough-riders." To his most intimate friend, he lamented his chances in life. "It is no use saying that I would like a chance at something I thought I could really do; at present I see nothing whatever ahead. However, there is the hunting in the fall, at any rate."

Hunting was a proxy for true battle. A decade later, he was still looking for a war to fight. On March 19, 1895, he wrote to New York's Governor Morton, ostensibly about a bill to remodel public schools, but it is his postscript that stands out: "In the very improbable event of a war with Spain I am going to beg you with all my power to do me the greatest favor possible; get me a position in New York's quota of the force sent out."[5] He claimed as his military credential three years of experience as captain in the state militia (he was not above padding his vita). "I must have a commission in the force that goes to Cuba!" And then he grumbled, "But of course there won't be any war." A year later, he would write to Anna: "I always hate words unless they mean blows."[6]

He whined to his sister about the job on the Police Commission because words there rarely came to blows: "There is nothing of the purple in it; it is grimy . . . inconceivably arduous, disheartening and irritating."[7] He faced the hostility of Democratic Tammany Hall on one side and the New York Republican machine under Thomas C. "Boss" Platt on the other, amid what he saw as the "folly of the reformers" and "the indifference of decent citizens, all under the foolish set of laws." The Great Heat Wave of 1896 — the mirror image of the Great Blizzard of 1887 — hit New York City, and Roosevelt was powerless — as he had been in the Dakotas — to do anything to break the destructive force. "The death-rate trebled until it approached the ratio of a cholera epidemic; the horses died by hundreds, so that it was impossible to remove their carcasses," he lamented from Oyster Bay.[8] He had ice distributed throughout the city; little else could relieve the suffering.

That same summer, Roosevelt felt the heat of literary scorn from reviewers in England who chastised him for chauvinism in the fourth volume of *The Winning of the West.* A squib in the *Athenaeum* on August 29, 1896, began in praise, "He is a man of culture, he is a sportsman of repute, and he has made his mark as a practical, patriotic, and incorrupt politician."[9] With all those laurels—man of culture, sportsman, patriot— Roosevelt moaned to George Putnam, "I wish I could persuade the general public to take a broader view of me as a historian!"[10] The reviewer attacked his tendency, as a historian, "to pander to vulgar passion and prejudice" against Great Britain, and Roosevelt sneered to Lodge that the reviewer was in a "perfect yell of rage."[11]

By the end of 1896, the police commissioner was lunching with Civil War general "Cavalry" Wilson and journalist Charles A. Dana about the prospect of his becoming the secretary of the United States Navy. With that job in mind, Roosevelt diplomatically softened his tone, advising Lodge to spur legislation that would call for the independence of Cuba, words that would obliquely call for war with Spain. Relaxing in a post-holiday letter to Anna, Theodore characterized himself as "a quietly 'Cuba Libre' man," assuring her, "There would not in my opinion be very serious fighting; and what loss we encountered would be thrice over repaid by the ultimate results of our action."[12] On April 19, 1897, Theodore Roosevelt became the assistant secretary of the United States Navy, and as he settled into his new job, he continued to drum up his case for fighting in Cuba. Writing to the head of the National Guard, Colonel Francis Vinton Greene, on September 15, he pleaded his case for fighting with them, claiming that he had served three years in the militia. He proposed that they raise a regiment with Greene as colonel and himself as lieutenant colonel. "I don't suppose there is any chance of the need arising," he demurred, "but I want to take time by the forelock so as to have my plans all laid and be able to act at once in case there is trouble."[13]

It is astonishing to look at his diary or read through his letters and try to imagine how he packed his days with so many disparate ideas and seemingly unrelated tasks. During the summer of 1897, even as he encouraged the historian Admiral Alfred Thayer Mahan to intercede with Secretary John Davis Long to build more battleships and as he fielded payments to the torpedo boat engineer Nathaniel Greene Herreshoff, the assistant secretary was negotiating a deal for his second book of essays, *American Ideals.*

The now-established writer worked to free himself from Putnam and to identify with the more impressive and perhaps more lucrative Harper & Brothers, whose magazine was publishing works by such writers as Theodore Dreiser, Horace Greeley, Winslow Homer, William Dean Howells, Henry James, Jack London, John Muir, Mark Twain, and Frederic Remington. He began by writing to Brander Matthews on June 10: "You spoke to me once about publishing a volume of essays. I fear I am bound to Putnam's, but I will frankly say I would much rather publish them in your series than anywhere else."[14] With his bank account in mind, he asked about the "money arrangements" at Harper's. The next letter from his pen that day went to G. P. Putnam's Sons as he tried to wiggle out of his longtime commitment to them. Mr. Putman had asked for political essays, and Roosevelt explained that his bundle of essays were not all, strictly speaking, political.

Consider what he has to say about the nature of his writing: "Moreover, my essays shade off so that it is hard to say when they are merely political and when they are what might be called politico-social."[15] Politico-social was a classification he had used in his book *New York* to designate prestigious clubs, including the Knickerbocker, the Union, the University, and the Union League. His literary voice blended genres in ways that conversation flowed in places like the Knickerbocker: "My reviews of the books of Pearson, Kidd and Adams come under that last head. I find it impractical to separate in two sets." He read widely and synthesized ideas without being fussy—this is a political essay and that a book review. "Now, if you think it unwise to publish the volume of essays in the way I have indicated I want you to say so frankly, and without the least hesitation." By July 1, with the bundle of essays in the mail, he still struggled to beg off: "I would of course rather have it go out by your firm than any other, but if you feel that it is inadvisable to try it, it might be that Harpers' would care for it in the series of volumes of essays by Brander Matthews, Cabot Lodge and others, which they are now publishing."[16] Be frank, he commanded, even as he angled for more money on the book.

Putnam's published *American Ideals* in October 1897, and the author, who was his own best publicist, sent a copy to William Allen White, author of "What's the Matter with Kansas?," an attack on William Jennings Bryan that McKinley's supporters had found useful in the presidential campaign. White was a perfect reader for *American Ideals*: "I don't know anyone," Roosevelt gushed, "who has fought more valiantly or more faithfully than you have fought to bring about the realization of some of these ideals; and so I want to have the pleasure of sending you the little volume."[17] In his *Autobiography* (1946), White wrote a colorful sketch of their first meeting: "He sounded in my heart the first trumpet call of the time that was to be. . . . I was afire with the splendor of the personality that I had met. . . . I had never known such a man as he, and never shall again. He overcame me."[18] Such vivid depictions of Roosevelt's charisma —a trumpet call, a fire—can be found in diverse memoirs of his friends and even acquaintances. He knew instinctively how to pitch his ideas.

Theodore Roosevelt's first crack at collecting essays for republication in a book had been *Essays on Practical Politics* in 1888, consisting of two essays on civil service that had been published in *Century Magazine*. The book offered him a forum to respond to his political critics, whom he labeled ignorant and imperfectly educated. At the heart of his critique was the power of language itself. The question he asked is a good one, even today: Who is doing the writing about the workings of government?

> The practical politician, who alone knows how our politics are really managed, is rarely willing to write about them, unless with very large reservations, while the student-reformer whose political experience is limited to the dinner table, the debating club, or an occasional mass-meeting where none but his friends are present, and who yet seeks, in pamphlet or editorial column to make clear the subject, hardly ever knows exactly what he is talking about, and abuses the system in all its parts with such looseness of language as to wholly take away the value even from such of his utterances as are true.[19]

It comes as no surprise that he argued for the precision and power of language as he urged politicians to take up the pen.

The man who is doing the work, Roosevelt professed, ought to be the man who is doing the writing, turning deeds into words and then words into deeds. The man of learning, although he may well be a man of wealth, ought to be a man of action. He quoted Joseph Choate, who put the blame for the corruption of the Gilded Age on the reticence of educated men to perform their political duties. Certainly, the scion of the Roosevelt family was laying the ground for his life in the political arena.

Writing the preface to *American Ideals* at Sagamore Hill in October 1897, Roosevelt struggled with words. He much later would confide to the young scholar Hermann Hagedorn that the preface laid out the philosophy of his public life. He wanted to show that a man who is an idealist could be practical in his idealism. The language of the preface flashes:

"These essays are written on behalf of the many men who do take an actual part in trying practically to bring about the conditions for which we somewhat vaguely hope; on behalf of the under-officers in that army which, with much stumbling, halting, and slipping, many mistakes and shortcomings, and many painful failures, does, nevertheless, through weary strife, accomplish something toward raising the standard of public life."[20] His prose comes to vivid life.

The final paragraph of the preface sounds familiar to anyone who knows Roosevelt's voice: "We feel that the doer is better than the critic and that the man who strives stands far above the man who stands aloof, whether he thus stands aloof because of pessimism or because of sheer weakness." Using the metaphor of a football game, he gives the victory, no matter the score, to the player who 'hits the line hard.' Certainly, that was the man he wanted to be. The arena is the place of action, as he would reiterate over the years, culminating in his "Man in the Arena" speech in 1910 at the Sorbonne:

> It is not the critic who counts; not the man who points out how the strong man stumbled or where the doer of deeds could have done them better. The credit belongs to the man who is actually in the arena, whose face is marred by dust and sweat and blood; who strives valiantly; who errs and comes short again and again; who knows great enthusiasms, the great devotions; who spends himself in a worthy cause; who at the best, knows in the end the triumph of high achievement, and who, at the worst, if he fails, at least fails while daring greatly so that his place shall never be with those timid souls who neither know victory nor defeat.

It is hard to find words that more forcefully define Roosevelt's political philosophy or, for that matter, America's sense of itself.

In the first essay of *American Ideals*, "Colleges and Public Life," Roosevelt urged the young, educated man to become a practical idealist, one who "must stand firmly for what he believes, and yet he must realize that political action, to be effective, must be the joint action of many men, and that he must sacrifice somewhat of his own opinions to those of his associates if he ever hopes to see his desires take practical shape" (35). The young, raw politician was inherently a pragmatist. Twenty years later, John Dewey would call that political philosophy simply "practical idealism."

American Ideals, the first in a lifelong string of sociopolitical books, set the man of words in a clear direction, establishing him as a newspaper writer and a literary critic and a political leader. He would publish hundreds of articles and reviews and editorials during his literary career in such places as *Harper's, Century, Scribner's, Metropolitan*, the *Forum, Outlook, McClure's, Atlantic Monthly*, the *Ladies' Home Journal*, as well as *Putnam's Monthly* and the *Kansas City Star*. Magazine editors paid him for his writing; and after that first publication, in what he considered a popular forum, he selected essays for a second publication in a book, for him a more dignified and lasting place for his words. Dual publication allowed him and his publishers to make money a second time. Fifteen volumes of such essays would appear over the course of his career, building on the ideas and language in *Essays on Practical Politics* and, especially, *American Ideals. The Strenuous Life* followed in 1900; *Addresses and Presidential Messages of Theodore Roosevelt, 1902–1904* (for which he took no royalties); *Outlook Editorials* in 1909; both *American Problems* and *The New Nationalism* in 1910 as he eyed another run for president; two more volumes, *The Conservation of Womanhood and Childhood*, and *Realizable Ideals*, in 1912, the year he ran on the Progressive ticket as a "Bull Moose"; *History as Literature* in 1913, with his address as president of the American Historical Association, and that same year *Progressive Principles*; and during the war years, *Fear God and Take Your Own Part* in 1916, both *The Foes of Our Own Household* and *National Strength and International Duty* in 1917, and *The Great Adventure* in 1918. We hear in these essays his strongest literary voice, increasingly strident, bullying from any pulpit he could find.

Reading *American Ideals*, we note the words of the title itself; as he put it to John Hay, "Don't let them bluff you out of the use of the word 'American.' I don't [think] anything better has been done than your calling yourself the American Ambassador and using the word American instead of United States."[21] To be an American was to swallow the whole of the Americas, North and South, for the United States. Roosevelt meant to claim the title for his government, his culture, and especially himself. He sang that note in the lead essay, "True Americanism": "We shall never be successful over the dangers that confront us; we shall never achieve true greatness, nor reach the lofty ideal which the founders and preservers of our mighty Federal Republic have set before us, unless we are Americans in heart and soul, in spirit and purpose, keenly alive to the responsibility implied in the very name of American, and proud beyond measure of the glorious privilege of bearing it" (18). In erasing any trace of immigrant origin, Theodore Roosevelt declared himself not a Dutch-American but an American-American and never tired of making the joke, "to be a first-class American is fifty-fold better than to be a second-class imitation of a Frenchman or Englishman" (22).

All along, Theodore Roosevelt was a reader who interacted with fellow writers and artists. Perhaps the writer he found most contemptible was fellow New Yorker Henry James; remember that his brother William James had been Theodore's professor at Harvard. The battle with Henry first surfaced in the 1884 presidential campaign when Theodore expressed loathing for a compatriot who would "bolt" from his country to pose as a "second-class imitation" of an Englishman. The *New York Times* reported a speech he gave to a group of Young Republicans: "Mr. Roosevelt said that his hearers had read to their sorrow the works of Henry James. He bore the same relation to other literary men that a poodle did to other dogs. The poodle had his hair combed and was somewhat ornamental, but never useful."[22] We can hear the derisive laughter around the room as Theodore warmed to the caricature of Henry as a poodle. The "mugwumps" or "bolters," who were irritated with the nomination of Republican James G. Blaine that year and supported the Democrat Grover Cleveland, looked to him like poodles of the "Henry James order of intellect." "They were possessed of refinement and culture to see what was wrong, but possessed none of the robuster virtues that would enable them to come out and do the right." Later, getting wind of the attack, James sniffed to Grace Norton: "What was Roosevelt's allusion to, or attack upon, me, in his speech? I have heard nothing, & know nothing, of it. I never look at the American papers."[23] Theodore was still deriding Henry a decade later in an essay "What Americanism Means," published in the *Forum* in April 1894. "Our nation is that one among all the nations of the earth which holds in its hands the fate of the coming years. We enjoy exceptional advantages, and are menaced by exceptional dangers; and all signs indicate that we shall either fail greatly or succeed greatly." Such lines are quintessentially Rooseveltian.

What may sound strange to us in the twenty-first century is that he took absolutely seriously the role of literary voices in a democracy. "Joel Chandler Harris is emphatically a national writer; so is Mark Twain. . . . They write as Americans for all people who can read English." Cosmopolitan aloofness signaled weakness, and he was especially hard on intellectuals like Henry James: "The failure of course being most conspicuous where the man takes up his abode in Europe; where he becomes a second-rate European, because he is over-civilized, over-sensitive, over-refined."

The essay moves in on James: "Thus it is with the undersized man of letters who flees his country because he, with his delicate, effeminate sensitiveness finds life on this side of the water crude and raw; in other words because he finds that he cannot play a man's part among men." A single punch might have done it, but Roosevelt pummeled away: second-rate, over-civilized, over-sensitive, over-refined, undersized, effeminate. Little wonder that James bridled at the caricature.

Although James claimed to be aloof from scorn, his review essay, "Democracy and Theodore Roosevelt," in the British journal *Literature* belies his pose: "Mr. Theodore Roosevelt appears to propose—in *American Ideals and Other Essays Social and Political*—to tighten the screws of the national consciousness as they have never been tightened before."[24] Not only does he tighten the screws, according to James, but he also narrows the vision: "The best he can do for us is to turn us out, for our course, with a pair of smart, patent blinders." Roosevelt forces himself on his constricted reader. "It is 'purely as an American,' he constantly reminds us, that each of us must live and breathe. Breathing, indeed, is a trifle; it is purely as Americans that we must think, and all that is wanting to the author's demonstration is that he shall give us a receipt for the process." James concluded that Roosevelt was a "very useful force" in advocating reform of the civil service and the New York City police, but his voice was "impaired for intelligible precept by the puerility of his simplifications."[25] It turns out that Henry James, too, was good in the arena and could return blows with words—impaired, unintelligible, puerile, simple.

Other American artists were more to Roosevelt's taste, most especially Frederic Remington, who had illustrated *Ranch Life and the Hunting-Trail*. In September 1897, Roosevelt invited Remington to join a naval inspection of the White Squadron: "I can't help looking upon you as an ally from henceforth on in trying to make the American people see the beauty and the majesty of our ships, and the heroic quality which lurks somewhere in all those who man and handle them."[26] Roosevelt wanted to do for the seas what his writings had done for the West; and he bullied his friends to get onboard. He wrote again to Remington on November 11 after an evening with Leonard Wood: "There were some naval men in too, including Bob Evans and Sampson, the Captain of the *Iowa*, and we were all wishing that you would do something about the Navy some time. We don't want you to forsake your old love, but just devote a wee bit of attention to another."[27] As it was soon to turn out, Remington would join such devotees to cover the Spanish-American War for the *New York Jour-*

nal and illustrate the confusion of battle, most famously in *The Scream of Shrapnel at San Juan Hill* (1898). The Rough Riders would acknowledge their gratitude to "the Colonel" on September 13, 1898, when the war was over, by giving him a bronze reproduction of Remington's *Bronco Buster*, a gesture that recognized military and artistic genius.

Also in September 1897, Roosevelt read *Talks on the Study of Literature*, a collection of Lowell Institute lectures given in the fall of 1895 by MIT professor of English Arlo Bates, and dropped him a note to say that, for the most part, he agreed with the literary critic, "though I have always had a dreadful mental limitation about the first and most popular part of *Robinson Crusoe*, and about a good deal of the *Arabian Nights*."[28] He joked that no one else in the household agreed with him. What especially caught his approving eye was the way Bates denounced "decadent" writers: the Belgian playwright Maurice Maeterlinck, the Norwegian playwright Henrik Ibsen, the French poet Paul Verlaine, and Leo Tolstoy. Roosevelt hoped that the American novelist William Dean Howells would take such notice, and he then added to the list the English novelist George Meredith, and the English novelist and poet Thomas Hardy, whose novels "beginning with *Tess* show distinct symptoms of the same disease." Roosevelt would continue this lament about the grim and sordid depictions of life in the late nineteenth century; he would still be railing against the fiction of Thomas Hardy in letters written during the last months of his life. In the letter to Bates he put in a good word for the poetry of Henry Wadsworth Longfellow and the novels of Sir Walter Scott. "However, I may be a crank about this," he noted, aware of his most human of tendencies. He thanked Bates for giving him "a number of most pleasant hours" of reading, and we note that Roosevelt lingered over the book's eighteen chapters.

Most biographers stress Roosevelt's uncanny speed as a reader with eidetic memory, someone who could thumb through pages of books, articles, especially reports at a very fast pace, recalling detail and even reciting passages of prose and poetry years later. The truth is that he read at different speeds depending on time and pressure and inclination. He spent a number of hours reading *Talks on the Study of Literature*, for instance. Roosevelt often savored books, taking time to think them over, rereading favorite passages, sometimes aloud with his wife and children, and on occasion stopping midstream to write the author a note of appreciation. In the fall of 1897, he wrote an adoring note to Jacob Riis, reminding him how influential a writer he had been. "When I went to the Police

Department it was on your book that I had built, and it was on you your-self that I continued to build."[29] And the next day, October 26, he wrote to the Chicago journalist and novelist Stanley Waterloo, who had just pub-lished *The Story of Ab*. We learn, here too, a good deal about Roosevelt's reading habits: "I have not read more than a third of the book yet, but that I have been interested in it may be proved from the fact that I have been reading it in the intervals of my regular work during the day; and I am a rather hard-worked man."[30]

We see the assistant secretary of the navy, plotting to strengthen the fleet and pining to see combat, and at the same time, or in the interstices, settling into his chair, book in hand. He lingered over the language and chatted, here with the author himself, about the ideas. His letter to Water-loo goes on to weigh the power of fiction: "The ways of primitive man have always been of all-absorbing interest to me, and I have come to the conclusion that it is only the good novelists who can teach us the best part of history—the history of life itself." He compares *The Story of Ab* to the trilogy of historical novels set in seventeenth-century Poland/Lithuania —*With Fire and Sword*, *The Deluge*, and *Fire in the Steppe*—by the Pol-ish novelist Henryk Sienkiewicz. We note that three years later, in the fall of 1900, Roosevelt would be reading Jeremiah Curtin's translations of Sienkiewicz's novels (not *Quo Vadis*, which he didn't like) and sending a message through Curtin that was meant for the novelist: "If you ever write to him I wish you would tell him how much comfort he gave a vice-presidential candidate in the midst of an exceedingly active campaign and also tell him that I had a regiment of men in the Spanish war whom I think would have been esteemed very competent fighters even by the as-sociates of Zagloba and the Knight of Boglets!"[31]

As Theodore Roosevelt moved from job to job, nothing stood in the way of his pen. Even when he was taking up the navy job, unlike any-thing he had previously done, and moving his family over the course of some months back to Washington, and looking for ways to supersede his boss, Secretary John Davis Long, and reading what came to hand, Roo-sevelt continued to write. He looked back over his years as police commis-sioner and published "Municipal Administration: The New York Police Force" in the *Atlantic Monthly* in September 1897. Purportedly working under Secretary Long, he wrote "The Naval Policy of America as Out-lined in Messages of the Presidents of the United States, from the Begin-ning to the Present Day" for the *Proceedings of the United States Naval Institute*, also published that year. Responding to Long's irritation with

THEODORE ROOSEVELT

his outspoken call for more battleships and torpedo gunships, Roosevelt ostensibly kowtowed to his boss: "Hereafter I shall adopt exactly the rule you suggest about my official publications, and about my general utterances also."[32] Then in an audacious riposte, he sent a copy of the article to President McKinley with the crucial caveat, "On the first page, where I speak of the need of strengthening the Navy, the words 'in my own opinion,' were put in at the suggestion of the Secretary."[33] It turned out that the young man was ill suited for the job of assistant secretary or assistant anything.

Continuing his writing and editing for the Boone and Crockett Club with George Bird Grinnell, Roosevelt used similar tactics to wield power over the text. "Beyond one or two slight verbal changes," he mollified Grinnell, "I have nothing serious to suggest about the preface, excepting on one point."[34] Yet his ostensibly mild revision grew to pages and pages on the nature of political policy and power. Outgoing president Cleveland in a proclamation on February 22, 1897, established thirteen forest reserves in the Pacific Northwest (twenty-one million acres in all), leaving the considerable task of bringing the proclamation to life in the hands of incoming president William McKinley. Roosevelt wanted Grinnell's sentence tweaked to give McKinley more credit. And he advised Grinnell to put more stress on the hunting of big game: "The big game will vanish, and only the pioneer hunters can tell about it." And while he was on the topic, he urged Grinnell to put in at least a paragraph on the destruction of the buffalo, a loss close to his heart in the 1890s. And then, later in the month, he admonished Grinnell for not writing books of his own. "They would be worth a hundred times as much as dry-as-dust pedantic descriptions by Shufeldt [the honorary curator of the Smithsonian Institution] and a lot of other little half-baked scientists."[35] Scientists "do good work; but, after all, it is only the very best of them who are more than brickmakers, who laboriously get together bricks out of which other men must build houses. When they think they are architects they are simply a nuisance." Nothing about the young writer and reader signaled restraint.

On his thirty-ninth birthday, October 28, 1897, Theodore thanked Anna for sending him a richly bound book: "You were just too good to send me for my birthday that very thing I wished; indeed the only thing I wished; and in such handsome binding."[36] They were a family of readers who reveled in literature wrapped in lush coverings.

His last child, Quentin Roosevelt, arrived unexpectedly early on November 19, and the proud father gushed, "By the aid of my bicycle I just got the Doctor & Nurse in Time!"[37] He was a romantic at heart, choosing a family name, but also the name of Sir Walter Scott's eponymous hero *Quentin Durward* (1823). Breathlessly, he bragged to friends that he had entered Quentin for Groton, the elite boarding school in Massachusetts founded in 1884 by the Episcopal clergyman Endicott Peabody. And then, settling into an armchair, Theodore read Emerson Hough's *The Story of the Cowboy* (1897) and sent an admiring letter to the *New York Evening Post* editor (and first editor of the *Nation*) Edwin Lawrence Godkin to be passed on to the writer, advising him on what to read: "I hope the writer likes some of Owen Wister's sketches as much as I do. 'The Pilgrim on the Gila,' for instance, and 'The Second Missouri Compromise,' give certain phases of western life as they have never before been given."[38] Hough would join the Boone and Crockett Club and later campaign for Roosevelt as a Progressive.

Not stinting on advice that day, Roosevelt wrote the captain of the Harvard football team Norman Winslow Cabot to buck him up after the loss to Yale when the Harvard team removed the *H* from their uniforms in humiliation. "At any rate, I feel that the team made an entirely creditable showing, and if the men don't get discouraged, and go in just as heartily next year with perhaps a trifle more attention to aggressiveness in attack, we will have good reason to expect a triumphant season."[39] He coached with his pen, "I want to see Harvard play hard, snappy football in attack." While president, he would be ever more involved with the sport, as John J. Miller has covered in *The Big Scrum: How Teddy Roosevelt Saved Football*.[40]

Later in the week, he wrote to the British explorer and big-game hunter Frederick Courteney Selous, who had been in the American West to kill wapiti, prong buck, and blacktail and whitetail deer, offering his regrets about missing the hunt. Then he gave Selous a reading list, including *The Story of the Cowboy*, Theodore S. Van Dyke's *Still Hunter*, and Washington Irving's *Trip on the Prairie*, along with portions of the books he and Grinnell had edited for the Boone and Crockett Club.[41] The same day he wrote to another British friend, the historian and politician James Bryce, thanking him for the gift of his book *Impressions of South Africa* (1897). "I am up to my ears in work at present," he explained, appending a handwritten line: "There is nothing I more wished than this very book you have sent me."[42]

A high mark of Roosevelt's reputation as a writer came that fall in an invitation from Augustus Lowell, sole trustee of the Lowell Institute in Boston and father of the poet Amy Lowell, to deliver a course of lectures in 1898 on "The Western Movement of the American People." "The number of lectures would be six, would it not?" Roosevelt queried.[43] "Will you also tell me what the compensation is?" He was not a man of leisure, "able to do whatever he wished," but a political appointee and a family man who was, after all, earning cash. He was thrilled with Lowell's suggestion, "that is, treating the ranch life as the last feature in the great epic of the western expansion of our race." The Lowell stage provided a perfect place to trumpet his experiences in the West, the dangers and hardships and "curious charm," as the culmination "in extremely abbreviated form" of a stage of civilization that had taken other peoples many centuries to accomplish. Under Roosevelt's pen, that is to say, the American experience, a variation on his own manic behavior, signaled the triumph of human civilization. Faster is not only faster, it is better.

Ironically, or maybe fittingly, the very day he accepted the offer from Lowell, December 7, 1897, Roosevelt wrote to Sylvane Ferris that he intended to sell off his cattle, assuming that the dwellings would have little value, and end his ranch business in the summer of 1898. In the Lowell lectures, his experiences in the Dakotas would find their way into the history of the nation; his deeds would be secured by words. Ranch life, for him, would become history.

And in another letter that arrived only two days later, his hunting prowess made its way into words, as well. The American zoologist Clinton Hart Merriam, in "Cervus Roosevelti; A New Elk from the Olympics," in *Proceedings of the Biological Society of Washington*, named what he called a species of elk "Roosevelt's Wapiti": "It is fitting that the noblest deer of America should perpetuate the name of one who, in the midst of a busy public career, has found time to study our larger animals in the native haunts and has written the best accounts we have ever had of their habits and chase."[44] Roosevelt swelled with pride: "To have the noblest game animal of America named after me by the foremost of living mammalogists is something that really makes me prouder than I can well say." Here, too, his hunting secured for him a life in language.

On December 13, 1897, he had nearly finished reading Owen Wister's *Lin McLean* and wrote to say that he had passed the book along to Cabot Lodge—without having quite finished it, we note. "I like not only the individual sketches, but the book as a whole," he enthused, saving his criticism for their next chat and looking forward to seeing the sketch "A Virginian" expanded—it would appear in 1902 as the novel *The Virginian: A Horseman of the Plains*. The next day, he wrote to his Harvard friend and Southwest Indian rights advocate Charles Fletcher Lummis, urging him to write an article about the use of Spanish terms in the West; he was especially keen to know the roots of the term "horsewrangler" (it probably came from the Mexican *caballerango* or stable boy, the *-erango* imperfectly echoed in "wrangler").[45]

On December 28, 1897, Roosevelt wrote again to Remington, thanking him for praising *The Winning of the West*, "the piece of work of which I am prouder than anything else I have done."[46] And then he returned the favor by praising Remington's *Crooked Trails* (1898). "Are you aware, O sea-going plainsman, that aside from what you do with the pencil, you come closer to the real thing with the pen than any other man in the western business?" Among those men, he included Grinnell and Wister and Hough, and then he compared Remington's strength as a writer to Rudyard Kipling's. Most tales of the West, even very good ones, "will die like mushrooms, unless they are the very best," he cautioned, but the very best — and he placed Remington's work in that category — "will live and will make the cantos in the last Epic of the Western Wilderness, before it ceased being a wilderness." He singled out Remington's account of a "bronco Indian, atavistic down to his fire stick; a revival, in his stealthy, inconceivably lonely and bloodthirsty life." That is a high literary calling for these popular writers who were, to Roosevelt's mind, creating the last cantos in the epic of the American West. It comes as no surprise that he slipped himself onto that stage, pointing out the best sections of *The Winning of the West* and then shamelessly asking, "Do you know my *Wilderness Hunter*?" A writer's life, we note, is full of vanity.

As Edith suffered from a mysterious illness in January 1898, Theodore reluctantly gave up traveling to New York for a Boone and Crockett dinner, the first one he had missed. He insisted in a letter to Christopher Grant La Farge, "I should like to have some say about the literary part of any book we publish."[47] As it turned out, the dinner was not well attended; and Roosevelt sent "a kind of wail of protest" in February. It had been a mistake to put the requirements so high that valid hunters were excluded for not killing the prescribed range of game animals. "I can't see any earthly reason for not taking all of the good fellows we can," he all but shouted, sounding very much like the president he was soon to become, the champion of a "square deal."[48]

On January 13, 1898, smelling conflict with Spain in Havana, Roosevelt pledged to New York adjutant general C. Whitney Tillinghast, "If there is a war I, of course, intend to go"[49] For his military experience, he claimed three years in the New York State militia, "not to speak of having acted as sheriff in the cow country!" And that same day, he wrote again to Colonel Greene, "I must ask you to let me know just as soon as possible if I can go under you as one of your majors. I am going to go somehow." The next day, he warned his boss, "if we should drift into a war with Spain and suddenly find ourselves obliged to begin it without preparation," the blame would be on the Department of the Navy.[50] Over pages and pages, he laid out a battle plan that called for a "flying squadron" of warships and more ammunition and men.

Being Theodore Roosevelt, he pledged to George Putnam "to break the back of the next two volumes of *The Winning of the West* or at least the next volume over the upcoming summer months."[51] By way of excuse, he offered, "I am a very busy man here." No kidding. Edith's illness worsened, little Ted showed signs of psychological breakdown, and Theodore ordered in a pile of books from the book dealer Rowland Ward: *Three Years' Hunting and Trapping in the Canadian North-West* by J. Turner-Turner; *The Far Interior* by W. Montague Kerr; *Travels in the Interior of South Africa* by James Chapman; *Sport on the Pamirs and Turkestan Steppes* by Major Cumberland; *A Naturalist in the Transvaal* by W. L. Distant; *Camping in the Canadian Rockies* by W. D. Wilcox; *Highlands of Kashmir* by Henry Zouch Darrah; and *Elephant Hunting in East Equatorial Africa* by Arthur H. Newmann. As antidote to pacing and worrying, the patriarch settled into a chair, book in hand, reading one hunting narrative after another.

The big battle before him, the one he had been hoping for all his adult life, was taking shape in Cuba. At anchor in Havana Harbor, on the evening of February 15, 1898, the United States battleship *Maine* mysteriously exploded and sank, killing 260 navy personnel. "Remember the Maine," screamed headlines in William Randolph Hearst's *New York Journal* and Joseph Pulitzer's *New York World* as President McKinley worked to calm the waters. The assistant secretary picked up his pen to craft words that would nudge Secretary Long to ready the navy for battle with Spain. To his Harvard Porcellian friend Benjamin Harrison Diblee, he raved, "Being a Jingo, as I am writing confidentially from one Porc man to another, I will say, to relieve my feelings, that I would give anything if President McKinley would order the fleet to Havana tomorrow. This Cuban mess ought to stop."[52] And he wrote again to General Tillinghast, pleading to be called upon to go to war in Cuba: "Pray remember that in some shape I want to go."[53]

Edith's misery did not lift, even as she gave up nursing baby Quentin, and her husband grew increasingly alarmed about her health. Alice, who was the child most like her father, was sent to Anna in order to calm the household, and a Baltimore physician, Dr. Osler, was called in but failed to be of help to Edith. Theodore worried over a New York City tax bill of $5,000 (10 percent of his estimated wealth of $50,000), claiming that he did not owe it because he lived in Oyster Bay—a fairly pedestrian irritation during tax season; he eventually paid the tax in order to secure his right to vote in New York (an issue that would come back in his run for governor in the fall). Reading an essay, "How Germans Become Americans," he wrote to its author, Ernest Bruncken, "To me the problem of Americanization, which is, to a large extent, the problem of the amalgamation and assimilation of the different race strains in this country, is the most interesting of all problems."[54] Then he detailed his own fusions of race: Lowland Scots, Dutch, French Huguenot, and Gaelic. The American experiment, to his mind, succeeded in the second generation as the English language predominated and religious difference softened.

On March 5, a gynecologist examined Edith and called for surgery to remove a benign abscess in her pelvic muscle, leaving an open wound and painful recovery. In a handwritten postscript to a letter to Brooks Adams, Roosevelt broke his usual silence about acknowledging fear: "Mrs. Roosevelt has been very, very sick all winter; for weeks we could not tell whether she would live or die. At last she was put under the knife; and now, very slowly, she is crawling back to life."[55] All the children, including Ted with his nervous disorder, were sent away from the house as the couple endured the wretched winter, both knowing well that death could take a mother from her family.

The truth is that Edith's husband could not get his mind off Cuba and the chance to put his own life in danger. It is interesting to note that he asked about whether his life insurance would cover him if were to die in Cuba. On March 8, he insisted in a letter to General Tillinghast: "I don't want to be in office during war, I want to be at the front."[56] Even then, he wanted to be in charge once he got to Cuba, and so he asked for advice about how to raise his own regiment. On March 15, he moaned to William Astor Chanler, "I shall chafe my heart out if I am kept here instead of being at the front."[57] He had already made contact with the army surgeon and "tremendous athlete" Leonard Wood about putting together a team of fighters. As he was dreaming up military strategies for defeating the Spanish fleet, he kept a keen eye on their torpedo gunboat *Temerario*.

On March 25, he met with Charles Doolittle Walcott, director of the Geological Survey, and looked at photographs of flying machines designed by Samuel Pierpont Langley, an old man by this time and secretary of the Smithsonian Institution. Roosevelt urged his boss to consider the possibility of building military flying machines for battle in what he could see was the next arena of war; he could have no idea that his own baby Quentin would command such a flying machine in the First World War and die in battle just months before the armistice.

Theodore, as he had told his sister, often felt like a caged animal, most especially when he was bored and bridled. His letters in the early months of 1898 record the fluctuations of his mood, frantic to see battle and anxious to ease the worry of his wife. Close friends and family, fretting over his bellicosity and seemingly suicidal tendencies (his brother Elliot's death from suicidal alcoholism in 1894 was perhaps most in their minds), wrote letters of concern. He defended himself in a series of letters, all echoing lines he first wrote to William Sturgis Bigelow, a physician and collector of Japanese art:

> I say quite sincerely that I shall not go for my own pleasure. On the contrary if I should consult purely my own feelings I should earnestly hope that we would have peace. I like life very much. I have always led a joyous life. I like thought, and I like action, and it will be very bitter to me to leave my wife and children; and while I think I could face death with dignity, I have no desire before my time has come to go out into the everlasting darkness.[58]

He assured his brother-in-law Douglas Robinson that his motives were not selfish, and his tone carried no levity, but, "I have a horror of the people who bark but don't bite."[59] Theodore's insistent mantra—"I like life"; "I could face death"; "I have no desire"; "I have a horror"—is still troubling to read in these letters. Little wonder that people close to him worried about his psychological poise.

On April 4, Roosevelt ranted to Major William Austin Wadsworth: "I would give a large sum, though a poor man, to have the running of our national affairs for just three days to come! You can bet nobody could stop the wheels afterwards!"[60] Here we have a vision of the Theodore Roosevelt who frightened party bosses on both sides of the aisle. He would soon have the running of our national affairs for far more than three days, and stopping the wheels would be nearly impossible for anybody, most especially for him.

On the same day, he admitted to his Harvard friend and American diplomat Robert Bacon, "This may seem almost strained language to you; but I can only repeat that you can scarcely imagine the bitter indignation which one grows to feel at a time like this."[61] The strain in his voice continued: "We can take no blood money for our murdered men, nor can we higgle and barter and submit to arbitration." He reported having used such language at a meeting with President McKinley and his cabinet: "I don't think my attitude has been misunderstood." No doubt about that. He spearheaded a telegram campaign to urge the government toward war —a version of Twitter campaigns today—that irritated the president. Roosevelt may have said more than he intended in a note to William Tutor: "I have preached the doctrine to [President McKinley] in such plain language that he will no longer see me!"[62] To Elihu Root, who would go on to be secretary of war in the second McKinley administration and then in Roosevelt's, he compared support of Cuban independence from Spain to the massacre of Armenians after European powers refused to protect them. Following an editorial in the *Sun* that urged the assistant secretary to stay at the Navy Department and not go to the war, Roosevelt wrote to the editor Paul Dana, listing his reasons for turning his words into blows: "I don't want you to think that I am talking like a prig, for I know perfectly well that one never is able to analyze with entire accuracy all of one's motives."[63] He was right about that.

On April 25, as war was declared on Spain for the liberation of Cuba, the U.S. Congress authorized three regiments and invited Roosevelt to lead one. He ceded power to Leonard Wood and accepted the commission as lieutenant colonel in the First United States Volunteer Cavalry. The politician worked quickly to bring together an odd assortment of men from the Rocky Mountain states and the state of New York that would be called the "Rough Riders." The one thing all the men had in common was their loyalty to Theodore Roosevelt—it was a regiment that called together men from all his experiences. With a coming military memoir in mind, Roosevelt returned to diary writing on Saturday, April 16, 1898, giving him a place to voice his impatient scorn for President McKinley and Secretary Long. Blasting through pages without regard for dates, he scrawled: "The President still feebly is painfully trying for peace. His weakness and vacillations are even more ludicrous than painful. Long is at last awake; and anyway I have the Navy in good shape." His pen turned, "But the army is awful. The War Dept is in utter confusion."[64]

His letters show how a man born into the wealth of the Gilded Age pre-

THEODORE ROOSEVELT

pared for military service. On April 28, he wrote to John Moore, "My regiment of mounted riflemen will probably be mustered in at San Antonio. Will you do me a great favor? I would like a couple of good, stout, quiet horses for my own use. They must not be gun-shy; they must be trained and bridlewise—and of course no bucking or anything of the kind."[65] And to his tailors at Brooks Brothers in New York City, he telegrammed an order for his clothes: "Ordinary cavalry lieutenant colonel's uniform in blue Cravenette," a fabric treated to make the uniform water-repellent. He thanked his brother-in-law Douglas Robinson for sending a Waltham watch, one he would use in battle to gage precisely what he would call his "crowded hour." Someone else had sent him the very spurs he wanted.

He thanked William Sewall for offering to fight, confiding in his old ranch partner that Admiral Dewey was in Asia because of Roosevelt's own doing and agreeing that Spain and Turkey were "the two powers I would rather smash than any in the world."[66] In a May 4 telegram to Joseph Lincoln Steffens, who wanted to publish the "swellest names" in the regiment, the Colonel could swell with pride: "Think it would be a little bit bad for the men to say which they were, but there are a number of Knickerbocker and Somerset Club as well as Harvard and Yale men going as troopers, to be exactly on a level with the cowboys." The Knickerbocker Club sent five and Harvard a dozen fighters, clean-cut and stalwart. The Colonel and his troops were one and the same.

Even with the men in place, he worried to Corinne, "I feel rather like a fake at going; for we may never get down to Cuba."[67] The next day he wrote to her husband, "Will you write Sylvane [Ferris] to get anything he can for the ranch, or to take it for anything he chooses to give?" In a PS, he instructed Robinson to pay the $500 on the policy, no doubt his life insurance policy. With his personal life in order, he wrote a note of gratitude to Secretary Long, together with his letter of resignation for President McKinley. And to his diary, he finished out the day: "Commissioned as Lt. Col., 1st U.S. Volunteer Cavalry. Wood as Col., by his choice. The Colonelcy was offered me."

Clearly this diary was meant for posterity. Increasingly, he would want his future readers, and here we are, to see history from his coign of vantage. On May 7, he continued his rant over the delays and stupidities in the War Department: "Against a good nation we should be helpless." The diary skips to Thursday, May 12, 1898: "Start for San Antonio, 10 pm." He reached camp on Sunday, the fifteenth, and could report four days later, "The drilling is incessant, & the progress of the regiment wonderful." His idea of joining the Harvard and New York men with the cowpunchers was working "capitally." Of the larger national effort, he sputtered, "There is no head, no energy, no intelligence in the War Dept. The President is of course really to blame." And yet, under Wood's command, the Rough Riders pulled together by May 26, "armed, mounted & drilled," and started for Tampa, Florida, by train on May 29. The railway system, it turned out, didn't work any better than the War Department; the men spent their time loading and unloading horses because of breakdowns and delays. By Friday, June 3, the train reached Tampa "in the wildest confusion."

Along the top of the page, he added, almost as a postscript, "E. came down for 4 lovely days." Even with Edith, who was fully recovered, at his side to calm him, the lieutenant colonel flashed, "No words can paint the confusion. No head, a breakdown of both the railroad & military systems of the country." Although his men were drilling impressively on horseback, there was no concerted effort toward reaching Cuba with those horses. Writing outside the lines of the diary, Roosevelt reported, "No allotment of transports. Utter confusion." The transports were ordered to stand still on May 9 and 10 and 11 and 12, and under the tropical sun, the men onboard were enervated. They weighed anchor on Monday, May 13, for Key West in continued confusion and there were ordered to convey another transport on May 18. Roosevelt could not believe the disorder. "This is simply idiotic. We cannot help the other transport in any way, as we have no tow-rope and any faster towing would sink the vessel." Any man who knew how to sail, much less studied naval vessels, would understand the folly.

But on Monday, June 20, he would write simply, "Reached Santiago," and by Wednesday, "Landed," and Thursday, "Marched," and on Friday, "Fight. . . . Lost 60 men killed & wounded, 20 slight," and by Saturday, "Rested." Over the next several days, the regiment moved forward. On Friday, July 1, the lieutenant colonel scribbled in pencil, "Rose at 4. Big battle, commanded regiment. Helped extreme front of firing line." The next entry is brief and nearly illegible, "Under shell & rifle fire." At a later time, in ink, Roosevelt recorded the losses, naming one man after another. It didn't take long to bring the Spanish to heel. On Sunday, July 3, he penciled in "truce at noon. Spanish fleet destroyed," and on Monday, "truce. Mismanagement horrible. No head to army." Days later, he recorded another bombardment and "truce again" on Monday, July 11, and finally on Sunday, July 17, "Surrender of Santiago." By the time the Rough Riders shifted camp into the foothills, Roosevelt reported to his diary that half his men were dead or disabled by wounds or sickness, mostly yellow fever.

The tone of the diary, by this time, lightened as the writer worked on material for his book. On Monday, July 25, he noted "Lost my hat in the creek," clearly a cue. And he recorded the joke of a soldier named Pollack: "'Do'n't want to wear my hair long and look like a wild Indian in civilized warfare.' Deep voice." Over the next week, he sketched names and oddities, for example, "Happy Jack who had fought for the light weight championship. His belief that Providence would not let him catch yellow fever from the old woman he helped." By Saturday, August 20, he could note, "Cuba safe."

Over those same months, from May, when his adventure started in San Antonio, to August, his letters home vary in tone and detail as he tells the Cuban war story to his friend Cabot Lodge, his editor Robert Bridges, and his children, wife, and sisters. To Lodge, on May 19, he had crowed, "Here we are working like beavers."[68] In his most characteristic voice, he bragged, "The troopers, I believe, are on the average finer than are to be found in any other regiment in the whole country." Eastern gentleman cooked and washed dishes for a company of troops from New Mexico, and Indians turned out to be excellent riders and pretty good fellows. He joked that his horses were so thin that he might have to kill and eat them. And he admitted being pretty homesick. With authorship most in mind, he wrote to Bridges, the man he had promised, "If I come back, you shall have the first chance at anything I write."[69] His letter on May 21 set the terms of the negotiation. Both *Century* and the *Atlantic Monthly*, he claimed, were after him for the story. If yellow fever or a Mauser bullet didn't get him, he wanted to publish his story of the war in magazine form, "that is, in popular form," and afterward in a book "as a permanent historical work."[70]

He wrote letter after letter, singing high notes. One to his children on June 6 stands out for what he reveals about social class in times of war. His favorite horse is Texas, and the camp has two pets, a jolly dog Cuba and a mountain lion kitten (an eagle named Roosevelt was added later). In Tampa, Edith is staying at a big hotel outside of camp, and at night the piazzas are festive with throngs of officers. He gives his children the assurance that his servant is doing a good job: "Marshall is very well, and he takes care of my things and of the two horses."[71] No gentleman would go to war without his body-servant, and Marshall, who was according to Roosevelt "the most faithful and loyal of men," was an old soldier in the Ninth (Colored) Cavalry. Theodore Roosevelt always had an African American valet; that would be true even at his deathbed in 1919 as James

Amos cared for him. His letter the same day, June 6, to Corinne is more intimate: "It has been delightful to have Edie here for the four days. . . . Col. Wood has let me be with her at the hotel from before dinner until after breakfast each day."[72] From the few surviving letters at the time, we know that in Florida the Roosevelts spent nights together in an elegant Moorish hotel, commandeered by the U.S. Army, in "a comfortable room with a bathroom."[73] Roosevelt delighted in the conjugal visit, as did his wife. Edith wrote home, "We were both very hungry for our supper, and glad to get to bed at once."

By June 10, the crowing was over in his letters to Lodge. "No words could describe to you the confusion and lack of system and the general mismanagement of affairs here." Everything going into Tampa, troops and equipment and food, all traveled on a single train track without switches or side rails. His regiment went twenty-four hours without food and, more alarmingly, without guidance of any sort about a transport into Cuba. "We had to hunt all over the dock among ten thousand people before, by chance we ran across first one and the other, and each regiment had to seize its transport and hold it against all comers; nothing but the most vigorous, and rather lawless, work got us our transport."[74] Even then they were ordered from Washington not to start. "We are in a sewer; a canal which is festering as if it were Havana harbor," he described his disgust. The officers stayed in the cabin of the steamer, while the men were crowded onto the deck and into the lower hold, "which is unpleasantly suggestive of the Black Hole of Calcutta." And the horses had it worse, embarked and then disembarked "for the simple reason that they began to die." What he wanted to impress on Lodge was the need for Washington to lead the troops into battle. In a postscript, he wrote, "One man should be in absolute control here, with autocratic authority."

Letters followed to Corinne and Anna, with whom he could be witty. "Why in the name of Heaven we should have been put on the transports before sailing I cannot tell. However, I won't complain if only we *do* start and get into the fun."[75] His letter to Lodge on June 12 was even more revealing. "Naturally this is not a letter that can be shown to anyone."[76] Then he instructed his friend about other fights to come, in the event that he would not live to make the argument himself: "You must get Manila and Hawaii; you must prevent any talk of peace until we get Porto Rico and the Philippines as well as secure the independence of Cuba." And then to his family by way of a note to Douglas Robinson, he assured them that the officers were quite well and that the troops were disciplined, though "wild with eager enthusiasm. Those of us who come out of it safe will be bound together all our lives by a very strong tie."[77]

For Theodore Roosevelt, war was a hazing into manhood. In letters to her husband, Edith called him "darling 'pigeon'" and let him know that their son Ted was especially keen on the idea of battle: "Ted hopes there will be one battle so that you can be in it, but come out safe. Not every boy has a father who has seen a battle."[78] Theodore was not the only one in his household who believed in war as a rite of passage. As his transport, the *Yucatan*, steamed southward "through a sapphire sea, wind-rippled, under an almost cloudless sky," he trumpeted to Corinne, the band played "The Star-Spangled Banner" and "The Girl I Left behind Me": "But it is a great historical expedition, and I thrill to feel that I am part of it."[79] He detailed the fight at Las Guasimas on June 25 that lasted a brisk two and a half hours, with the loss of a dozen men and another sixty wounded. Beyond the battle, he reported to his sister that he slept on the ground in the same clothes for four days and drank without boiling his water. Here we find the beginnings of the nature writing he would include in the book: "We have a lovely camp here, by a beautiful stream which runs through jungle-lined banks. So far the country is lovely; plenty of grass and great open woods of palms . . . with mango trees."[80] Yet even as they buried their dead, singing "Rock of Ages," he watched the vultures wheeling overhead ready to pluck out the eyes and tear the faces of the dead Spaniards, and then he spotted the land crabs, gathering in gruesome rings around the dead. That was the first skirmish.

By July 3 from outside Santiago, Roosevelt wrote briefly to Lodge that for three days he had been at the "extreme front of the firing line; how I have escaped I know not; I have not blanket or coat; I have not taken off my shoes even; I sleep in the drenching rain, and drink putrid water."[81] In memos to Colonel Wood, Roosevelt detailed battles along the way, even one that left him scrambling. "It was after we had taken the first hill — I had called to rush the second, and, having by that time lost my horse, climbed a wire fence and started toward it. After going a couple of hundred yards, under a heavy fire, I found that no one else had come."[82] To Lodge, the next day, he shouted, "Not since the campaign of Crassus against the Parthians has there been so criminally incompetent a General as Shafter." Little wonder that Lieutenant Colonel Roosevelt, rushing from one hill to another, felt that in terms of command, he was truly alone in Cuba.

The war essentially over, Roosevelt looked for his laurels. To Lodge, he blustered, "Gen. Wheeler says he intends to recommend me for the medal of honor; naturally I should like to have it."[83] And again on July 10, "I think I earned my Colonelcy and medal of honor, and hope I get them; but it doesn't make much difference, for nothing can take away the fact that for the ten great days of its life I commanded the regiment, and led it victoriously in a hard fought battle." And, unable to keep his pen at bay, he swooned, "I do not want to be vain, but I do not think that anyone else could have handled this regiment quite as I have handled it during the last three weeks."[84]

Words had become blows, and now the blows flowed into words. The letters to Lodge in July 1898 came close to the stories he would tell in *The Rough Riders*. "However, enough of grumbling. Did I tell you that I killed a Spaniard with my own hand when I led the storm of the first redoubt? Probably I did. For some time, for your sins, you will hear from me a great many 'grouse in the gunroom' anecdotes of this war."[85] He had anecdotes galore. As the troops lay in wait, a Lieutenant Haskell took a wound to the stomach; another man stood to salute and fell with a bullet in his brain.

"But then came the order to advance, and with it my 'crowded hour'; for there followed the day of my active life." The day stood vividly in his mind, a blend of memory and imagination.

When he had read versions of the War of 1812, the historian in him recoiled from firsthand accounts, often written in what he called "the 'hurrah' order of literature," and yet here he was after Kettle Hill singing his own hurrah notes in the letter to Lodge, notes he would use over and over in the book.

> At the head of the two commands I rode forward (being much helped because I was the only man on horseback) and we carried the first hill (this was the first entrenchment carried by any of our troops; the first break in the Spanish line; and I was the first man in) in gallant shape and then the next and then the third. On the last I was halted and for 24 hours I was in command, on the extreme front of the line, of the fragments of the six cavalry regiments, I being the highest officer left there.

After the battle victory, the men still standing — over half of them had been killed or wounded or set upon by yellow fever or dysentery — were in tatters like a band of tramps. Lieutenant Colonel Roosevelt wrote to thank Douglas Robinson for sending him a box of medicine and fresh underclothes and asked him to check with Brooks Brothers on his order for an extra pair of breeches and gaiters. He wanted Edith to order his

THEODORE ROOSEVELT

shoes, a stout pair to replace the ones rotting on his feet. After considering his health and appearance, he could not resist telling his brother-in-law, "By the way, I then killed a Spaniard myself with the pistol Will gave me which was raked up from the *Maine*."[86] Single-handedly, he avenged the sinking of the *Maine*. His hope, incredible as it sounds, was to bring the surviving troops together, four thousand strong, to carry the battle on to Puerto Rico.

Reports of the fighting by Richard Harding Davis in the *New York Herald*, among others, made Theodore Roosevelt wildly popular. By the end of July, the lieutenant colonel was being wooed by New York state senator John Lewis Childs to run on the Republican ticket for governor of New York. Sorting out his motives for going to battle, he explained to Douglas Robinson, "It makes me feel as though I could now leave something to my children which will serve as an apology for my having existed."[87] And as he waited in Santiago for an order to continue fighting in Puerto Rico or to take the Rough Riders, who were suffering mightily from yellow fever, to Montauk for six weeks of recovery, news came from Cabot Lodge that Theodore Roosevelt had secured his commission as colonel. He swelled with pride that he could leave his children with an honorable name.

The Colonel was eying political possibilities with his usual sardonic wit. "The good people of New York at present seem to be crazy over me; it is not very long since on the whole they felt I compared unfavorably with Caligula," he quipped to Lodge. The average New York boss willingly bankrolled politicians in the trivial matters of war and expansion, "provided you don't interfere with the really vital questions, such as giving out contracts for cartage in the Custom House and interfering with the appointment of street sweepers."[88] The Rough Riders decamped in Montauk as the Colonel embraced the idea of a run for the governorship. "If I am not nominated, I shall take the result with extreme philosophy and with a certain sense of relief, and shall turn my attention to the literary work which is awaiting me."[89] Even as he was elected governor of New York in the fall 1898 election and prepared to take office in January, Theodore Roosevelt continued to tell the story of the war that made him a man. Robert Bridges, then the assistant editor of *Scribner's Magazine*, remembered, "When he returned from the Spanish-American War and landed in Montauk, he sent word to the magazine that he wanted to talk about his proposed story of 'The Rough Riders.'" As they sat together on the lawn at Sagamore Hill in the late summer of 1898, "It was all perfectly clear in the Colonel's mind. He knew the grand divisions of his story, although he had not written a line." After Roosevelt's election as governor in November, Bridges asked again about the publishing schedule, a seemingly impossible feat for a busy political man, only to be assured that every manuscript promised would be delivered on time.

The Rough Riders was Theodore Roosevelt's best book because it brought together all his talents and inclinations as a writer, allowing him to write in every genre he had mastered: military history, ornithology, nature writing, and hunting narrative. The painstaking scholarly details of *The Naval War of 1812* and battles and intrigues of *The Winning of the West* are everywhere to be seen in the story of his Rough Riders as they gather the regiment, outfit and arm themselves, struggle for transports into Cuba, set up camps, and move into battle. The fact that the Colonel had no need of the Astor Library and could rely on his own diary and letters and memory, if not imagination, is a sign that this slim volume completed for him the winning of the West. He never returned to write the remaining volumes. He and his Rough Riders had gallantly won the final battle in the long saga.

The most remarkable passages in the war story sketch the natural world. As he moved into battle, with Sergeant Hamilton Fish in the lead, followed by Captain Capron's troop and then the Rough Riders under Leonard Wood, the action stops, astonishingly, as Roosevelt on horseback takes in the scene. "The tropical forest was very beautiful, and it was a delight to see the strange trees, the splendid royal palms and a tree which looked like a flat-topped acacia, and which was covered with a mass of brilliant scarlet flowers."[90] Here we see the young ornithologist, listening intently for the sounds he loved. "We heard many birdnotes, too, the cooing of doves and the call of a great brush cuckoo. Afterward we found that the Spanish guerillas imitated these birdcalls, but the sounds we heard that morning, as we advanced through the tropic forest, were from birds, not guerillas, until we came right up to the Spanish lines." Then Roosevelt turns his pen to the hunting stories he had been telling since a teenager. "It was very beautiful and very peaceful, and it seemed more as if we were off on some hunting excursion than as if we were about to go into a sharp and bloody little fight" (49). Once in the thrall of the hunt, Roosevelt describes incredible shots on both sides, bullets entering body after body, grim images of wounded and dead bodies open to vultures and land crabs.

As in other hunting tales, he moved comfortably—too comfortably for his sister Anna and Cabot Lodge—into the personal pronoun. Many critics of the book joke about his unruly use of "I"; as legend has it, Scribner's had to order more of the letter to complete the typeset for the book. Looking closely, we see that the writer deployed the pronoun for verbal effect, sounding down the page like a flurry of bullets from a Gatling gun. "I sprang on my horse. . . . I formed my men. . . . I started in the rear. . . . I speedily had to. . . . I had intended." They come faster and faster down the paragraph: "I found I should be quite unable to run up and down the line and superintend matters unless I was mounted; and, moreover, when on horseback, I could see the men better and they could see me better" (70–71). It took twenty-five of the offending pronouns to get him up Kettle Hill.

After finding no colonel in charge, Lieutenant Colonel Roosevelt took command, employing another twenty-three of the pronouns to get the job done: "'Then I am the ranking officer here and I give the order to charge'" (72–73). Soon after, as he had reported to Wood, he jumped over a wire fence and ran about a hundred yards and turned back, to see only five men actually following his lead. Retracing his steps and "taunting" his men bitterly, he discovered that in the fog of war, they simply had not seen him leading the charge. Three other men shouted, "'Lieutenant, we want to go with you, our officers won't lead us'" (77).

It is here, in the shortest sentence of the book, that Theodore Roosevelt finally shot his prey. "At about the same time I also shot one" (77). Oddly, at the moment of a hunter's greatest triumph, the kill shot, Roosevelt hesitates. He had never before and would never again kill human prey (although he himself would be hunted and shot later in Milwaukee). That brief sentence might have sufficed, and yet he could not stop his pen from making the bigger claim, one he had first bragged about in a letter to Douglas Robinson. "As they turned to run I closed in and fired twice, missing the first and killing the second. My revolver was from the sunken battleship *Maine*, and had been given me by my brother-in-law, Captain W. S. Cowles, of the Navy." Turns out that with one shot Roosevelt claimed revenge for the sinking of the *Maine*.

The Chicago satirist Finley Peter Dunne, in the guise of Mr. Dooley, an opinionated Irish American bartender, looked askance at Roosevelt's literary performance in *The Rough Riders*. "'Ye know I'm not much throubled be lithrachoor, havin' manny worries iv me own, but I'm not prejudiced again' books. I am not.'" Mr. Dooley good-naturedly begins his review, "'Whin a rale good book comes along I'm as quick as anny wan to say it isn't so bad, an' this here book is fine. I tell ye 'tis fine.'" Guilelessly, Dooley reads *The Rough Riders* as the story of one man, Tiddy Rosenfelt, in his battle with Spain, letting him speak for himself about his regiment:

> " 'I detarmined to raise wan iv me own,' he says. 'I selected fr'm me ac-
> quaintances in th' West,' he says, 'men that had thravelled with me
> acrost th' desert an' th' storm-wreathed mountain,' he says, 'sharin'
> me burdens an' at times confrontin' perils almost as gr-reat as anny
> that beset me path,' he says. 'Together we had faced th' turrors iv
> th' large but vilent West,' he says, 'an' these brave men had seen me
> with me trusty rifle shootin' down th' buffalo, th' elk, th' moose, th'
> grizzly bear, th' mountain goat,' he says, 'th' silver man, an' other fe-
> rocious beasts iv thim parts,' he says."

Dooley eyes the whole of Roosevelt's literary career and shrewdly reads *The Rough Riders* as yet another hunting story, not for buffalo or moun-tain goats this time, but for Spaniards, human prey. His literary asides are hilarious: Rosenfelt quoting the Bible from Walt Whitman and killing a commander "with a small ink-eraser." Finally, Tiddy Rosenfelt breaks free of the Rough Riders and bursts into battle all by himself: " 'This showed me 'twud be impossible f'r to carry th' war to a successful conclusion un-less I was free, so I sint th' arrmy home an' attackted San Joon hill." Amaz-ingly, the Colonel hunts the Spanish army with a lightweight .32 caliber hunting rifle and, even more amazingly, manages to win the war with a single bullet that tears through body after body:

> "Arrmed on'y with a small thirty-two which I used in th' West to
> shoot th' fleet prairie dog, I climbed that precipitous ascent in th'
> face iv th' most gallin' fire I iver knew or heerd iv. But I had a few
> rrounds iv gall mesilf an' what cared I? I dashed madly on cheerin' as
> I wint. Th' Spanish throops was dhrawn up in a long line in th' for-
> mation known among military men as a long line. I fired at th' man
> nearest to me an' I knew be th' expression iv his face that th' trusty
> bullet wint home. It passed through his frame, he fell, an' wan lit-
> tle home in far-off Catalonia was made happy be th' thought that
> their riprisintative had been kilt be th' future governor iv New York.
> Th' bullet sped on its mad flight an' passed through th' intire line
> fin'lly imbeddin' itself in th' abdomen iv th' Ar-rch-bishop iv Santi-
> ago eight miles away. This ended th' war."

Dooley gives the author, who had been elected governor of New York, the benefit of doubt: "An' if Tiddy done it all he ought to say so an' relieve th' suspinse. But if I was him I'd call th' book 'Alone in Cubia.'" Everyone laughed. Everyone.

From the governor's office in Albany, Tiddy fired a note straight to Dunne on November 28, 1899: "I regret to state that my family and intimate friends are delighted with your review of my book. Now I think you owe me one; and I shall exact that when you next come east you pay me a visit. I have long wanted the chance of making your acquaintance."[91] Roosevelt had ways of absorbing his critics, and liked a good laugh as much as anybody, especially one that made him the star. He wrote to Lodge, "Yes, I saw Dooley's article and enjoyed it immensely. It is really exceedingly bright. How he does get at any joint in the harness!"[92] Without bristling, he told Dunne that his Dooley articles "are not only as humorous bits of reading as I have ever read, but are also full of a very profound philosophy — which I suppose is always a mark of the real master of humor whose works are more than evanescent."[93] The governor could laugh and applaud Dunne because he was confident, for the first time, that he himself was a literary man.

Chapter 7
"Running in a Groove"

The work is necessarily confining, and prolonged confinement
and close occupation become irksome and debilitating to a man of
robust build and sanguine temperament, accustomed to being much
in the open air . . . yet with characteristic grit he has faced the ordeal
of authorship to such good purpose that a dozen works from his
pen have made their appearance within the last nineteen years.
{ Joseph B. Gilder, "A Man of Letters in the White House," 1901 }[1]

Colonel Roosevelt, as contributor for twenty years to Scribner's
Magazine, was one of the most thoughtful, considerate, and efficient
authors. When he promised a manuscript for a certain date,
that promise was kept absolutely, no matter what intervened.
. . . He was a busy man, but his literary work was just as
complete as though he had devoted his whole time to it.
{ Robert Bridges, *Theodore Roosevelt as
Author and Contributor*, 1919 }[2]

At the turn into the twentieth century as Roosevelt moved from one governmental job to another—assistant secretary of the navy, governor of New York, vice president of the United States—he held the promise of two "mistresses" in his hands. He was determined to write even as he ran for public office. The fame of his military adventures in Cuba propelled him into the governor's mansion, and fear of losing reelection in 1900 nudged him into the vice presidency on the McKinley ticket. "Cabot feels that I have a career," he boasted to his sister Anna. "The dear old goose actually regards me as a presidential possibility in the future."[3] To his cousin-in-law Alice Lee, he cautioned, "This popularity of mine is in its very nature evanescent."[4] Even as the public wooed him and fellow politicians plotted for and against him, Theodore Roosevelt knew he was also a literary man; thus it was that even in a confining office, he sought ways of putting pen to paper. The brash young assistant secretary of the navy had once bragged to George Putnam, "As soon as I get things running in a groove in this office, as I will in six months or so more, I want to begin to get the materials together for my next volumes of the *Winning of the West*. As you know, there are to be four of them."[5] One thinks hard about a phrase like "running in a groove" and wonders how anyone could sort out the machinery of a government office quickly and efficiently enough to turn his mind to writing scholarly history. The truth is that Roosevelt was always thinking about the place he might earn in American letters.

He was not alone in calculating the politics of the literary arena. The United States, even in it infancy, had yearned for cultural legitimacy, and over the nineteenth century various efforts toward founding an academy of writers and artists had sputtered and failed, until a sunny afternoon in September 1898 on the veranda of the Saratoga Hotel, where a meeting of the American Social Science Association was taking place. Henry Holbrook Curtis, a throat specialist, proposed to the ASSA president Simeon Baldwin, a federal judge, that their organization branch out into the arts and humanities. The model the men had in mind was the Institut de France, with its four academies, to display the depth and breadth of national erudition. From that conversation, the National Institute of Art, Science and Letters took shape under the leadership of Dr. Curtis and the writer Charles Dudley Warner, who had partnered most famously with Mark Twain to write *The Gilded Age: A Tale of Today* (1873). Yale American studies professor R. W. B. Lewis pointed out in his history of the American Academy of Arts and Letters that these efforts followed the November 1, 1897, opening of the elegantly designed Beaux-Arts-style Library of Congress in Washington, D.C. — a project first planned by John Adams and started with the book collection of Thomas Jefferson. A guidebook proclaimed, "America is justly proud of this gorgeous and palatial monument to its National sympathy and appreciation of Literature, Science and Art."[6]

America meant to be more than a political and commercial and military force in the world, and Theodore Roosevelt as he became the governor of New York and then the vice president and president of the United States yearned to be a vigorous voice in the American idiom. In 1898, he was selected as one of 150 founding members of the National Institute of Arts and Letters. By 1904, the members fashioned a more rarefied group, patterned after the Académie française, to be called the American Academy of Arts and Letters. Voting in the initial seven members from its own ranks, the Institute elected William Dean Howells and Samuel Clemens—a literary and cultural stretch by any measure. Others included the sculptor Augustus Saint-Gaudens; the poet Edmund Clarence Stedman; the painter John La Farge; the historian John Hay, who was also secretary of state to McKinley and later Roosevelt and, most famously, private secretary to Abraham Lincoln; and the composer Edward MacDowell. When the votes were counted, Henry James stood next in line. On January 7, 1905, those seven august members voted in another eight members, including novelist Henry James, architect Charles McKim, historian Henry Adams, art historian Charles Eliot Norton, sculptor John Quincy Adams Ward, Yale English professor Thomas Lounsbury, poet and novelist Thomas Bailey Aldrich, and president of the United States Theodore Roosevelt. The president was unusually young for this distinction; all but MacDowell were of his father's generation, men of a certain age and rank, and conspicuously all of them white Christian Protestants.

None of the young generation passed muster; no Stephen Crane or Frank Norris, both of whom died young; no Jack London or Upton Sinclair until 1944 (he resigned in 1966) or Theodore Dreiser that same year, but only an Award of Merit. All of these experimental writers would come, years later, to define the American voice that the Academy thought it was enshrining. Local-color realist Hamlin Garland was voted into the Institute in 1898 but did not make his way into the Academy until 1918. The young poet and protégé of President Roosevelt, Edward Arlington Robinson, came into the Institute in 1908 but not into the Academy until 1927. Robert Frost, also admired by Roosevelt, was voted into the Institute in 1916 but waited fourteen long years until members elected him to the Academy. Philosopher William James may have had it right when he sniped that the Academy looked to him like a schoolboy's game of "'we are in and you are out'" (20–21). He declined invitation. The line he will always be remembered for is packed with snark: "And I am the more encouraged to this course by the fact that my younger and shallower and vainer brother is already in the Academy." Sibling rivalry trumps about anything. The record shows that Henry didn't vote for his brother either time he was nominated.

The Academy squabbled over the acceptance of female members and in 1908 voted for the octogenarian poet Julia Ward Howe, if only to prove they were not sexists.[7] Henry Adams took to task the Academy secretary Robert Underwood Johnson, an increasingly brittle intellect: "Did it ever occur to you that if we put Julia Ward Howe on our membership lists, we are subject to much criticism for neglecting other women? I do not see how we justify omitting Edith Wharton, for example, and I've no doubt that a dozen more would claim much higher literary credit than Mrs. Howe can claim" (100). Academy members snubbed Wharton in 1908; she would become the next woman elected to the Academy, but not until 1930.

The "color line" was as real in the arts and humanities as it was in politics and society. Short story writer Charles Waddell Chesnutt and poet and novelist Paul Laurence Dunbar never appeared in the balloting. Certainly, no one nominated the writer and former slave Anna Julia Cooper. No mention was made of Booker T. Washington, the leading force for the advancement of African Americans, and the author of *Up from Slavery.* President Theodore Roosevelt would rely on him as the most prominent African American voice in politics at the turn into the twentieth century. But the Academy turned its back on women and African Americans and immigrant writers and Jews and Muslims because the cultural game was, in truth, "we are in and you are out." Not until after 1930, under the direction of the younger Henry Seidel Canby, did the Academy expand to include women, and not until the 1940s would they finally cross the "color line" in selecting sociologist W. E. B. Du Bois.

Late in life, Theodore Roosevelt would address the Academy, delivering a signature speech, "Nationalism in Literature and Art," on November 16, 1916, in New York City.[8] The undercurrent of his talk, it comes as no surprise, was the Great War raging in Europe and the failure of American troops to join that effort. The ostensible topic that afternoon was the nature and significance of American sculptors, architects, poets, historians, and philosophers. As Henry James had observed about the vociferous Roosevelt, he meant to screw writers and artists to the American land. "But if the art is genuinely national," Roosevelt declared, "the leadership must take advantage of the life of the people, and must follow the trend of its marked currents." The former president called for an amalgam of ideas and mixings of blood, and found in that flux genuine meaning. "This means that here in America, if we do not develop a serious art and literature of our own, we shall have a warped national life." "Warp" is a word that Roosevelt used often, meaning in this instance a distorted national life, twisted by the very fact that the culture had no imaginative life of its own. He embraced women writers, even using the Irish nationalist Lady Gregory to pitch his arguments for cultural authenticity. Slavishly paying homage to the art and literature of other civilizations and countries, he cautioned, merely acknowledges that other peoples have wielded the power of imagination. Only Americans, he thundered, could produce the real American thing: "Yet the fact remains that the greatest work must bear the stamp of originality. In exactly the same way the greatest work must bear the stamp of nationalism. American work must smack of our own soil, mental and moral, no less than physical, or it will have little of permanent value." He was not alone in calling for an American-American literature.

In that smacking of soil, we hear echoes of Ralph Waldo Emerson's call for intellectual independence in his 1837 Phi Beta Kappa address, "The American Scholar": "Perhaps the time is already come when it ought to be, and will be, something else; when the sluggard intellect of this continent will look from under its iron lids and fill the postponed expectation of the world with something better than the exertions of mechanical skill. Our day of dependence, our long apprenticeship to the learning of other lands, draws to a close." What could be more American than the very words "sluggard intellect"? As a boy on his family trip through Egypt, Tedie had met Emerson, by then an old man with what Corinne thought "a lovely smile, somewhat vacant."[9] We hear, too, the voice of Edgar Allan Poe in an 1842 review of Rufus W. Griswold's *The Poets and Poetry of America*: "That we are not a poetical people has been asserted so often and so roundly, both at home and abroad, that the slander, through mere dint of repetition, has come to be received as truth. . . . Because it suited us to construct an engine in the first instance, it has been denied that we could compose an epic in the second."[10] Certainly, Theodore Roosevelt heard the American epic in the writers of the West. He could very well have crafted Poe's language himself.

More than any other American voice in the nineteenth century, however, we hear in Roosevelt's prose the barbaric yawp of Walt Whitman in *Democratic Vistas* (1871). The poet flatly insists, "I say that democracy can never prove itself beyond cavil, until it founds and luxuriantly grows its own forms of art, poems, schools, theology." And being Whitman, he goes on:

> Our fundamental want to-day in the United States, with closest, amplest reference to present conditions, and to the future, is of a class, and the clear idea of a class, of native Authors, Literatuses, far different, far higher in grade than any yet known, sacerdotal, modern, fit to cope with our occasions, lands, permeating the whole mass of American mentality, taste, belief, breathing into it a new breath of

life, giving it decision, affecting politics far more than the popular superficial suffrage, with results inside and underneath the elections of Presidents or Congresses, radiating, begetting appropriate teachers and schools, manners, and, as its grandest result, accomplishing . . . a religious and moral character beneath the political and productive and intellectual bases of The States.[11]

Little wonder that historian Daniel Aaron considers Roosevelt's career a "Song of Myself."[12] What could sound more like Theodore Roosevelt's voice as he raised his fist and pushed his face, teeth and all, into a crowd?

In the 1916 address to the Academy, Roosevelt referred to Whitman as "a warped although rugged genius." We are left wondering, again, about the word "warped." Remember that Roosevelt could be squeamish about the demands of the body. He may have recoiled, reading, say, the fifth section of "Song of Myself" as the poet loafs with his soul:

> I mind how once we lay such a transparent summer morning,
> How you settled your head athwart my hips and gently turn'd over
>   upon me,
> And parted the shirt from my bosom-bone, and plunged your
>   tongue to my Bare-stript heart,
> And reach'd till you felt my beard, and reach'd till you held my feet.

Such lines may have been as vexing to him as the sexual longings of Anna Karenina. Once he opened a book, any book, Theodore Roosevelt was vulnerable to the force of language, a mark of what made him a good reader.

He admired the poet, and in his 1911 essay, "Dante and the Bowery," compared Whitman to Dante in his fearless depictions of the full range of human experience: "Of all the poets of the nineteenth century, Walt Whitman was the only one who dared use the Bowery—that is, use anything that was striking and vividly typical of the humanity around him —as Dante used the ordinary humanity of his day."[13] Sounding very like Whitman, Roosevelt argued that the Bowery contains multitudes: "The Bowery is one of the great highways of humanity, a highway of seething life, of varied interest, of fun, of work, of sordid and terrible tragedy." The problem, he thought, for Whitman was that his talents were greater than his poetry (that may be what he meant by warped), but, even then, Roosevelt complained that the poet was not as widely known as his poetry deserved to be.

In his office at Sagamore Hill, Roosevelt framed a copy of George Gardner Rockwood's 1871 photograph of Whitman, together with a manuscript fragment of *Democratic Vistas*, marked with Whitman's own revisions, that reads in part: "The genius of Democratic America demands something rough, very ample not [∧too] delicate [∧not thinly 'good,'] not too particular [∧and: fierce, rank]. . . . At present what is called literature is [∧appears to be] in the hands of a lot of thin-blooded [∧rose-scented-] gentlemen, quite & little better than dandies, gurgling." Whitman's words struck with force; Roosevelt, too, thought that American writers were thin-blooded, rose-scented, gurgling, like Henry James, literary poodles. The words "rough" and "fierce" and "rank" embody the vitality both men sought in American letters.[14] Whitman and Roosevelt imbibed the spirit of the young country and amplified their voices in patterns that have an uncanny resemblance.

As the Institute of Arts and Letters was coming into being in 1898, Colonel Roosevelt was affronting his military destiny in Cuba, and by the end of the summer returned in triumph from his battle as hordes of reporters and politicians, clamoring for him to run on the Republican ticket in the New York gubernatorial election, surrounded him and the Rough Riders in Montauk and followed him home to Sagamore Hill. He kept a guarded eye on his career as a writer. Military heroism sells well in America, and through his pen Theodore Roosevelt, even as he was overwhelmingly elected governor of New York, was poised to make even more money as an author. He was born into wealth by any standard other than that of Old New York—yet Theodore and Alice, and then Theodore and Edith, often struggled to make ends meet. His yearly salary as governor of New York was a considerable $10,000, along with a stately if somewhat stodgy mansion in Albany. Surprisingly, Edith and Theodore were able to save his salary because, for the first time, they were living well on his earnings as a writer.

Once he had his office "in the groove," implausible as it sounds, he wrote, or more precisely dictated, three books from the governor's mansion in Albany: the military memoir *The Rough Riders* (1899), the biographical sketch *Oliver Cromwell* (1900), and the politico-social collection *The Strenuous Life* (1900), made up of speeches he was giving as governor. *Scribner's Magazine* editor Robert Bridges, in *Theodore Roosevelt as Author and Contributor*, explained that Roosevelt turned to dictating articles and books (as he increasingly did his letters), relying on the steady hum of his voice.

"It was all perfectly clear in his mind," Bridges said of *The Rough Riders*. "He knew the grand divisions of his story, although he had not written a line." Thus the Colonel told the story of his heroism to Miss Ella Rawls, who "did her work excellently" and earned a letter of recommendation for "good and faithful work."[15] And he followed the same pattern of oral composition for his scholarly work. The stenographer who took his dictation for *Oliver Cromwell* told Bridges that the governor would appear in his study with some books of reference and a pad of memoranda. "Then he would complete a chapter of historical narrative which demanded a very careful knowledge of dates and places. This was not as easy as a narrative of personal experience." And yet the purported history, written without much attention to scholarly sources, had the look of a personal narrative. Roosevelt put the word count at fifty-two thousand, and added by way of explaining to Bridges what he meant by a history: "At any rate, it is not a rehash of anyone else's work, and it is not simply a series of annals." The biography came out first in serial form in *Scribner's Magazine* from January through June 1900, and then in a book. The British military attaché with the Rough Riders, Arthur Hamilton Lee, Lord Lee of Fareham, who was becoming Roosevelt's intimate friend, good-naturedly gibed that *Oliver Cromwell* was "a fine imaginative study of Cromwell's qualifications for the governorship of New York."[16]

Roosevelt was a literary maestro. According to Bridges, once he dictated a story in full, the typed text stood nearly complete; in his own hand he revised slight errors and added words, but the manuscript "could have been printed as it stood." As he had sought to do at Putnam's, Roosevelt orchestrated all the aspects of a publication, preferring illustrations in magazine articles but not many in book editions, where he thought the words ought to stand by themselves. The making of a book delighted him, the writing and revising and copyediting, even the cover, its design and the fonts, all done under his eye.

In Albany, the politician became more and more comfortable speaking in pulpits of all sorts, turning thoughts into speeches and speeches into articles and articles into books. He was learning the ropes as a national politician, pushing words into platitudes. His authorized biographer Joseph Bucklin Bishop, reading a set of his speeches, once complained that reading one of them would do it, and, besides, anyone who had been listening to the president already knew the platitudes by heart. "I can't talk anything but platitudes," the president retorted. "But platitudes and iteration are necessary in order to hammer the truths and principles I advocate into people's heads."[17] *The Strenuous Life* illustrates how Roosevelt hammered truths into people's heads. The essay that gives the book its title began as a speech before the Hamilton Club in Chicago on April 10, 1899. The governor warmed to an audience, and because in those venues his speaking voice had ready and eager listeners who laughed and cheered and applauded on cue, Theodore Roosevelt did his best composing, as a stenographer took down word after word.

The chapter was folded into a collection of essays about life in the public sphere, all appropriate for the presidential campaign in the fall of 1900, with Roosevelt stowed away in the vice presidency, a place where both party machines thought he could do little harm. The volume begins with lines from Alfred, Lord Tennyson's "Ulysses":

> How dull it is to pause, to make an end,
> To rust unburnish'd, not to shine in use!

He picked out lines he favored and ended with

> . . . for my purpose holds
> To sail beyond the sunset, and the baths
> Of all the western stars, until I die.

The other epigraph is in German from Goethe's *Faust*, who at the end of his life declares (in translation)

> Yes! to this thought I hold with firm persistence;
> The last result of wisdom stamps it true:
> He only earns his freedom and existence,
> Who daily conquers them anew.

Theodore Roosevelt had little trouble putting himself in league with Ulysses and Faust.

He seems utterly without irony in the first essay in proclaiming sloth as sin: "A life of slothful ease, a life of that peace which springs merely from lack either of desire or of power to strive after great things, is as little worthy of a nation as of an individual."[18] The book is a collection of earnest talks and essays he had been writing over the previous two years. "Admiral Dewey" was published first in *McClure's Magazine* in October 1899, and "Military Preparedness and Unpreparedness" in *Century* the next month, followed by "Fellow-Feeling as a Political Factor." In the March issue of *Churchmen*, he published a moral lecture, "The Best and the Good," and in the *Outlook* he pondered the connection between "Character and Success" and then "Promise and Performance." "Civic Helpfulness" appeared in the October *Century*, just before the successful fall election. He worked to sew his patchwork into a pattern, including even his address at the opening of the Pan-American Exposition, "The Two Americas." Nothing was left, not a scrap of his voice, on the cutting room floor.

The book came out in October of 1900, and he sent a copy to the British journalist John St. Loe Strachey, inviting him to read it and proudly detailing his sacrifice to his party by accepting the vice presidential nomination. "I have no expectation of going on any further in public life," he confided, "but it is all right anyhow, for I have succeeded in accomplishing or helping in the accomplishment of certain things which I deem important."[19] Another copy went to Arthur Lee, with whom he could be openly funny. Note his comic timing. "Now, my dear fellow, do not forget that the vice-president has no power and is really a fifth wheel to the coach. Also remember that it is not a stepping-stone to anything except oblivion. I fear my bolt is shot, but I have had a first-class time."[20] His bolt supposedly shot, he settled into the boredom of the vice presidency in the first months of 1901, whiling away his time reading books and magazines.

As a reader, he was more one of us than you may think. Without snobbery, he picked up just about anything, savoring the colloquial, the popular, the "cheap," the humorous, the regional, alongside the literary, the rarefied, the universal, the classical. University of Chicago professor Edward Wagenknecht in *The Seven Worlds of Theodore Roosevelt* (1958) described contemporary accounts of those who watched him read. On a busy morning in the hotel lobby, he would gather up all the newspapers and read them one by one over breakfast, tossing each page to the floor, leaving him surrounded in scattered piles of paper. While traveling by train, according to the journalist Oscar King Davis, Roosevelt always carried reading material, and as the train stopped, he would buy the new magazines, all of them. "The character of the magazine did not seem to make any difference to him."[21] He read a magazine from cover to cover, everything in it, and tore the pages out one by one, tossing them, as he did newspapers, to the floor around him. He thought of magazine and journal articles as ephemeral, not worthy of saving, and that was why gathering his own articles into books was so important to him. Books guaranteed future readers, and a legitimate place on shelves, both in private homes and public libraries.

Reading his letters, we see curious connections between the magazines and books he was reading and the political world around him. Take the

Irish American Tammany Hall boss Richard Croker, for example. After reading *McClure's Magazine* in February 1901, the vice president wrote a dazzlingly complimentary note to the Progressive Kansan William Allen White on his portrait essay "Richard Croker."[22] "How in the name of Heaven can you divine a man like Croker? Here you are living in a small town out in Kansas, not accustomed to the conditions of life in a seething great city, pay a somewhat hurried visit to New York; and yet you sketch Croker as no one in New York, so far as I know, could sketch him."[23] The imagination, Roosevelt knew well, is a powerful muscle. He kept Croker and White in mind as he continued to read.

By the spring of 1901, he had read and reread Wister's biography *Ulysses S. Grant* (1900). He wrote to his friend, trying to cast the book in its brightest light: "It seems to me that you have written the very best short biography which has been written of any prominent American. . . . It is very easy to write a second-rate short account of a great man, but it is the most difficult kind of historical writing to produce the best possible short account of a great man."[24] He may well have had his own work on *Oliver Cromwell* uncomfortably in mind. "Dan" Wister, who had been a freshman at Harvard when Theodore was a junior, was smitten by his friend even in college and always took pride in being a literary companion of such a charismatic man. Over his life Wister would be a dear friend to many writers, including Henry James, who had been a great friend of his mother's, and Edith Wharton, who adored being with him, and later Ernest Hemingway, who liked the guy if not his writing, as we shall see.

Theodore wrote Dan again on July 20, 1901, from Oyster Bay, where he had been reading Frank Norris's novel about bloody clashes between farmers and the railroad, *The Octopus: A Story of California*, the first in a planned trilogy that the author called his Epic of the Wheat. Norris, that is to say, was creating an epic about the American West, but Roosevelt wasn't so sure. "I read it with interest," he confided to Wister. "He has a good idea and he has some power, but he left me with the impression that his overstatement was so utterly preposterous as to deprive his work of all value."[25] Norris's lurid portrait of life in California did not mesh with Roosevelt's more prosaic experiences with farmers and ranchers and railroad men in the Dakotas, Wyoming, Idaho, Colorado, or New Mexico. It was realism and not naturalism that the vice president preferred and, at that, a realism he could recognize from his own experiences in the world. Literary naturalists, like Norris, depict life on the very edge, among the most vulnerable, where the social world breaks apart to expose life stripped of

THEODORE ROOSEVELT

its social layers and open to the brutalities of human nature. Characters in a naturalist novel are prey to every human depravity — all the seven deadly sins — and naturalist novelists are inclined to preach about social and economic conditions that cause deviant behavior. Roosevelt, even as he was honing his own preaching skills, was skeptical of Norris's.

The Octopus looked to him like the ravings of a political reformer, "half charlatan and half (dude) fanatic." Roosevelt was a witty man. Boss Croker was still on his mind. "It is just exactly as if in writing about the tyranny and corruption of Tammany Hall I should solemnly revive the stories of Mediaeval times and picture Mr. Croker as bathing in the blood of hundreds of babies taken from the tenement houses," he joked. He saved his best lines for friends like Wister: *The Octopus* "stands on an exact level with some of the publications of the W.C.T.U. [Woman's Christian Temperance Union] in which the Spanish War, our troubles in the Philippines, and civic dishonesty and social disorder, are all held to spring from the fact that sherry is drunk at the White House."

By 1901, Roosevelt was thinking about who should become his own biographer, who could best make his character shine. Richard Watson Gilder, the editor of *Century Magazine*, suggested that Wister write a presidential "Life." Roosevelt privately cautioned Gilder against the idea: "Do not speak to Owen Wister about it."[26] The president thought William Allen White, who could get under the skin of Boss Croker so convincingly, would do a better job on another New Yorker. "I have a kind of feeling that the man who is to write about me ought if possible to be a man who has lived near the rough side of things, and knows what it is actually to accomplish something — not just to talk about accomplishing it."

During 1901 Wister was working on the manuscript of *The Virginian* (1902), a book he would dedicate to the president. When Dan asked his friend and mentor to read and pass judgment on the manuscript, Theodore advised in the strongest possible terms that Dan rewrite one brutal scene; he wanted Balaam's beating of the horse that caused the horse's death to be interrupted by the Virginian who would save the horse's life. Other writers winced at the false note. The truth is that Wister wasn't much of a novelist. His only other significant novel, *Lady Baltimore* (1906), gave his literary friends all sorts of troubles; both Roosevelt and Edith Wharton counseled the novelist, more in private than in print, about flaws in his manuscript.

Much later, Dan Wister's young literary friend Ernest Hemingway, too, winced at his prose. After reading Wister's memoir, *Roosevelt: The*

Story of a Friendship, 1880–1919, published long after Roosevelt's death, Hemingway wrote the author from Piggott, Arkansas, on December 26, 1930, dictating the letter because he had broken his right arm. He groused about having to talk rather than write the letter. "What's meant to be read with the eye should be written with the hand and checked by the eye and the ear as it's written. Rhetoric or particularly involved sentences can be easily constructed with the mouth but they do not untangle so well with the eye."[27] Those are sentences worth reading again—the eye, the hand, the ear. Perhaps no better critique could apply to the writings of Theodore Roosevelt, who during the presidential years came more and more to rely on his spoken voice alone, without much regard to eye or hand or even ear.

At the heart of the letter, after all the whining, was Hemingway's critique of Wister's biography and how the portrait had failed. "I wanted to write you about the Roosevelt book but I couldn't because the way it worked out finally was that, (it seemed to me), a man must not write about another man of whom he has been very fond after that man is dead because it can not be done." Hemingway's voice struggled, "It is only by staying miles outside that you have any chance to recreate the person." The next day, Hemingway switched to pencil, scribbling with his left hand, and his mood lifted: "My god what tripe this letter is!" But he managed a postscript that turned his attack to the president himself for having ordered changes to the Balaam incident in *The Virginian*: "What was it about Balaam that Roosevelt made you take out? It was *that* made me *furious* against him." The pugnacious young novelist, whose prose followed Roosevelt's literary dictates—his words came from the American voice and embodied the ethos of the strenuous life—bristled at the president's literary bullying. To Hemingway, no politician ought to get in the way of literary art.

The most amazing thing we learn from reading Roosevelt's letters during his years as governor of New York and then president of the United States is the way that reading a book could influence his thinking about the world around him. Some books he read actually fueled his political ideas. To take the most vivid example, he had read *How the Other Half Lives* (1889) when he was police commissioner in New York City and had gone directly to meet the author Jacob Riis, whose depictions of urban poverty and whose relentless campaign to reform tenement house laws in New York stayed in the young man's mind. Over his two brief years as governor of New York, Roosevelt put into law Progressive reforms that Riis had called for in his exposé. The governor signed into law the Costello Anti-Sweatshop Act on April 1, 1899, for example, turning words into deeds in his call for the inspection and regulation of tenement houses. In the Amendment to the Labor Law, he called for inspection of and safety in the workplace, and for reducing working hours for women and children. He signed the Sabine Eight-Hour Act for state employees that mandated prevailing wages.

That wasn't all he did. The Ambler Dairy Products Acts removed artificial coloring from oleo-margarine unless the label itself told the truth, and he endorsed the same cautions on fruit juices. As a founding member of the Boone and Crockett Club, the governor called for the protection of forests and fish, signed the Hallock Bird Protection Act, and looked to the future of conservation by funding natural history and geography courses in the public schools. On April 18, 1900, he proclaimed that no person would be excluded from public schools on account of race or color, thus rejecting the idea of "separate but equal." For the same reason, however, he championed the compulsory mainstreaming of Native American children. The list goes on: a cap of 6 percent interest on loans; a state hospital for crippled children; seats for waitresses and women working in factories; a requirement that flax thread be a part of any fabric calling itself linen.

And then, because he was Theodore Roosevelt, he toured sweatshops with Jacob Riis on May 31, 1900, to see for himself if those words had become deeds. After he moved to Washington as vice president, on March 28, 1901, he wrote to Riis: "Of course, call me 'Colonel.' I would rather have that from you than any other title."[28] Riis was the writer most often invited to family dinners at Sagamore Hill, both men finding comfort in their friendship. In 1904, Riis wrote a biography, more a hagiography, *Theodore Roosevelt, the Citizen*, calling him "a brother." The book sold well during the presidential campaign that year. Years later, after Riis's death in 1914, the "Colonel" wrote in tribute, "I have loved him dearly and I mourn him as if he were one of my own family."

Roosevelt's letters tell us much about the writer as he moved at breathtaking speed into the White House after Leon Czolgosz's bullet killed President McKinley eight long days later, making Theodore Roosevelt the twenty-sixth president of the United States on September 14, 1901. Amid the turmoil of ceremony and official mourning, the young president thought about authorship. He dashed a sharp note of caution to Caspar Whitney, the editor of *Outing* magazine: "You have the deer articles herewith, but I shall get you to make it plain that they were written before I became President. I shall put a short 'foreword' in, and date it from the

Vice-President's Chamber, in June last. Let me see the proof; & mind, there must be no advertisement that 'President Roosevelt' has written anything. My name must only appear as it appeared for instance in *Scribner's*; no flaring business of any sort."[29] He meant to be president first and a literary man second, at least in the beginning. No flaring until he had that office "in the groove."

Chapter 8

A Literary President

There was always something imminent about him, like an
avalanche that the sound of your voice might loosen. The word
demanded by the occasion was instantly on his lips, whether it were to
give pleasure or pain. In his presence one felt that the day of judgment
might come at any moment. No easy tolerance with him, but you
could always count on the just word, the square deal, and
tolerance of your opinion if it were well founded.

{ John Burroughs, "Camping with President Roosevelt," 1906 }[1]

oosevelt had risen to the highest public office and meant, at
the start, to serve that single "mistress," but he was, after all, a
reader and writer by inclination. When he was bored by prosaic duties or overwhelmed by political pressures, the president indulged
in reading and rereading books of all sorts, favorite classics, dime novels,
contemporary fiction, histories, odd magazines that he picked up wherever he went. He cajoled writers, many of them scornful of the man and
his ideas, to join him at the White House. The president read their books,
sparred with them over dinner, and dazzled and unnerved them with his
restless energy and ominous power. Writers lampooned him — Henry
James dubbed him "Theodore Rex," Henry Adams "pure act," and Twain
a "Barnum" clown — but that didn't keep them away from his "court."

The president assumed office on September 14, 1901, and by October
16 invited the writer Booker T. Washington, whose *Up from Slavery* had
just come out, to join him at the White House. The year before, as vice
president, he had written to Harvard football coach William Henry Lewis,
whose parents had been slaves, about "the upward path" of race in America (he would appoint Lewis as the first African American U.S. Attor-
ney in 1903). "I wish I could meet Booker T. Washington and you, with
Paul [Laurence] Dunbar, and talk the matter over at length."[2] After becoming president, he invited Washington to dinner, setting up a firestorm

of criticism that would follow him throughout his career and, in some quarters, would continue to reverberate as Barack Obama moved into the White House in 2008 as the forty-fourth president of the United States. The White House had always been home to African American servants — indeed Theodore Roosevelt, a grandson of a southern slave owner, had black manservants. Henry Pinckney was the steward at the White House from 1901 to 1910; his son Theodore Roosevelt Pinckney was born during those years; and another son, Roswell (named for the plantation owned by TR's maternal grandfather James Bulloch), played with Quentin when both were young boys. Marksman and FBI agent James Amos served for twelve years as Theodore Roosevelt's valet and bodyguard and later wrote *Theodore Roosevelt, Hero to His Valet.* What offended a populace that condoned Jim Crow laws and rituals on both sides of the Mason-Dixon Line was not that a black man had entered the White House but that Booker T. Washington dined as a friend and with the First Family. The president's feisty voice is clear in a letter to another Harvard football coach, Lucius Nathan Littauer: "There are certain points where I would not swerve from my views if the entire people was a unit against me, and this is one of them. I would not lose my self-respect by fearing to have a man like Booker T. Washington to dinner if it cost me every political friend."[3]

Not every writer agreed with the president. A week later, on October 23, Roosevelt was at Yale to accept an honorary degree together with Mark Twain, whom he admired even as they sparred over the idea of democracy and the perils of expansionism. Twain remembered the encounter in his autobiography, in a segment he shielded from publication at the time: "The President asked me if I thought he was right in inviting Booker T. Washington to lunch at the White House. I judged by his tone that he was worried and troubled and sorry about that showy adventure, and wanted a little word of comfort."[4] The advice may be surprising. "I said it was a private citizen's privilege to invite whom he pleased to his table, but that perhaps a president's liberties were more limited; that if a president's duty required it there was no alternative but that in a case where it was not required by duty it might be best to let it alone, since the act would give offense to so many people when no profit to the country was to be gained by offending them." Twain actually counseled Roosevelt to observe the "color line," and the president stepped back only slightly. Washington was invited back to the White House on February 26, 1902, and many times over the years of Roosevelt's presidency for talks on southern politics and race but not over dinner.

Tom Sawyer and *The Adventures of Huckleberry Finn* were favorite novels of the president, who thought *Huck Finn* was a classic and would tuck both books into his "Pigskin Library" when he went game hunting in Africa after his presidency. But Twain was a bitter critic of the Colonel. On June 15, 1898, as Colonel Roosevelt was about to have his "crowded hour" on Kettle Hill, a group of writers joined folks from all walks of life in protesting the military campaign in Cuba and its ominous ripples into the Philippines and Puerto Rico and Guam, the very places Roosevelt wished to go next. The Anti-Imperialist League grew in number to twenty-five thousand, including writers who put their words to work against the bellicosity of President McKinley and Colonel Theodore Roosevelt. Notables included social settlement founder Jane Addams, short story writer Ambrose Bierce, philosopher John Dewey, humorist Finley Peter Dunne, novelists Hamlin Garland and William Dean Howells, philosopher William James, poet Edwin Arlington Robinson, and most vocally Twain, who proclaimed that he was "opposed to having the eagle put its talons on any other land."[5] Colonel Roosevelt, he mocked, "was in a skirmish once at San Juan Hill, and he got so much moonshine glory out of it that he has never been able to stop talking about it since."

The relentless voice of the Colonel rattled Twain, who read his braggadocio as a sign of immaturity if not insanity. He fumed to Andrew Carnegie: "Mr. Roosevelt is the Tom Sawyer of the political world of the twentieth century, always showing off; always hunting for a chance to show off; in his frenzied imagination the Great Republic is a vast Barnum circus with him for a clown and the whole world for audience; he would go to Halifax for half a chance to show off and he would go to hell for a whole one."[6] In a letter to his close friend Joseph H. Twichell, Twain struggled with ambivalence: "I knew I had in me somewhere a definite feeling about the President if I could only find the words to define it with."[7] The man had ways of disarming his critics with the touch of a hand. "Every time, in 25 years, that I have met Roosevelt the man, a wave of welcome has streaked through me with the hand-grip; but whenever (as a rule) I meet Roosevelt the statesman and politician, I find him destitute of morals and not respect-worthy." They were sometimes in company and behaved themselves; Twain was twenty-three years Roosevelt's senior and regarded the young man as dangerous because he was ready to kick the Constitution into the backyard whenever it got in the way.

The president's charisma bemused many writers, especially the old guard. On January 7, 1902, he hosted the annual diplomatic reception, a huge afternoon gathering, and invited his Lafayette Square neighbor Henry Adams to dinner in the evening at the White House, a place Adams had not been since 1878 when Rutherford B. Hayes hosted him and his wife, Clover, just before her suicide. The house was full of memories. Joining them for the evening was another neighbor, John Hay, who had served as private secretary to Abraham Lincoln and had agreed to stay on from the McKinley administration as Roosevelt's secretary of state, and Cabot and Nannie Lodge.[8] The men that evening were scions of the American elite, trained to be polite. As Edith Wharton's hero Newland Archer put it, they all "lived in a kind of hieroglyphic world, where the real thing was never said or done or even thought," at least not at the table. The "real thing" was held more closely, tightly in the fist, until it could spring its barbs. Before the dinner, John Hay had sniped to Henry Adams: "Teddy said the other day: 'I am not going to be the slave of the tradition that forbids Presidents from seeing their friends. I am going to dine with you and Henry Adams and Cabot whenever I like. But of course I must preserve the prerogative of the initiative.'"[9] The tone of that phrase, "the prerogative of the initiative," had stuck in their craw. Little wonder that the old men bristled at dinner.

Adams was never comfortable in Roosevelt's company. In a note to Elizabeth "Lizzie" Cameron, he critiqued the dinner, carping that the food was as bad as the service and the drinks (the Roosevelts served watered wine with meals). "Edith was very bright and gay, but as usual Theodore absorbed the conversation, and if he tired me ten years ago, he crushes me now."[10] As he listened, Adams traced the nuances of manners that evening. To Cameron, he lamented what she had often heard, "It is my creed now that my generation had better scuttle gracefully, and leave Theodore to surround himself with his own rough-riders." The vigorous president fit the new century, and Henry Adams felt, to put it mildly, superannuated. "That nervous tic I have so often told you of—the instinct to roll on the ground and pray to the dynamo, is becoming chronic here with me." For Adams, the dynamo had replaced the Virgin Mary as the wellspring of modern life, and the president embodied the turbine. In *The Education of Henry Adams*, Adams decreed Roosevelt "*pure act*" and confessed that "his first year of Presidency showed chronic excitement that made a friend tremble."[11] Adams worked to get at the heart of his irritation that Roosevelt had the audacity and dumb luck to be at the helm of a country once run by John Adams and John Quincy Adams. It was "his childlike and infantile superficiality with his boyish dogmatism of asser-

THEODORE ROOSEVELT

tion," Adams snapped to Cameron. "He lectures me on history as though he were a high-school pedagogue."

What were the old men to do with the frenetic young president? In public, Hay spoke about Roosevelt's honesty, bravery, intellect, and patriotism "tinged by the ineffable light which for want of a more descriptive term we call genius."[12] But behind his subject's back, Hay could be as wickedly witty as he was publicly charming. After another dinner, he chuckled to Adams that the president was in fine form: "He began talking at the oysters, and the *chasse-café* found him still at it."[13] He put his finger on the problem. "When he was one of us, we could sit on him — but who, except you, can sit on a Kaiser?" Who indeed!

Younger writers approached Roosevelt with less mockery and more hope. Hamlin Garland, the author of *Main-Travelled Roads* (1891), braved a letter to the president on May 5, 1902, requesting his help in solving flaws in the language of the Homestead Act, a law that had been crafted by President Abraham Lincoln, granting homesteaders 160 acres, whatever their situation and wherever the land. In stories of the Middle Border, Garland depicted the struggle of farmers to thrive on the meager land. Roosevelt had first heard of Garland a decade before through Brander Matthews, who was working on *A Study of American Literature* (1896) and grousing about Garland's more radical study, *Crumbling Idols* (1894). Roosevelt agreed with Matthews that Garland "is a man with some power and with half an idea, but he is such a hopeless crank that nothing can be done with him, I fear."[14] But then, he bought *Crumbling Idols* and read for himself Garland's call for literary "veritism" and "local color" as expressions of a genuine American voice, a "smacking of the soil." In a letter to Matthews, he agreed that Garland was "entirely in error" when he dismissed Shakespeare and Homer and Milton as crumbling idols: "I think that his ignorance, crudity, and utter lack of cultivation make him entirely unfit to understand the effect of the great masters of thought upon language and upon literature."[15] And he thought Garland's insistence on the power of "local color" in art was absurd: "I read Mark Twain with just as much delight, but with no more, whether he resides in Connecticut or in Missouri." But after venting to Matthews, Roosevelt invited Garland to lunch with Brooks Adams and then to have dinner with Cabot Lodge. "Be sure you don't fail me at either place," he mentored, "for both of them are men you ought to know."[16] He tendered his opinions without the bitterness of someone like Brander Matthews, who seemed to him a literary snob, "one of the men who mixes with 'our best circles,' where they look down on patriotism, and the plain everyday duties of decent American citizens."[17]

Garland's sinewy stories about disputes between homesteaders and speculators, who often squeezed out the little guy, made the case for changing the Homestead Act. Thus from the White House, Roosevelt wrote back to Garland on May 5, 1902, in a note marked "personal": "I shall have to take a little time about it, and probably get assistance from Congress, but it will be done."[18] Indeed it was. Representative Moses Kinkaid proposed a plan to expand the land grant to 640 acres in Nebraska, and the president would sign the revised Homestead Act in 1904. And he signed the 1902 Reclamation Act that funded irrigation projects in twenty western states to give homesteaders water rights. Politicians had the power to create the language of law that moved words into deeds.

Using the language of the Sherman Antitrust Act (1890), the president was working in 1902 to dismantle the nation's biggest trust, the newly forming Northern Securities Company. While campaigning on that issue in the fall election, Roosevelt spoke in Pittsfield, Massachusetts, on September 3, 1902, and as he traveled to Lenox, his barouche was hit hard by a speeding trolley car. Secret Service agent William Craig put his arm out to protect the president, was swept under the oncoming wheels, all eight of them, and his body lay torn and bleeding; he had been a favorite of the Roosevelt children, and was the first agent ever to die in the line of duty. The president, thrown thirty feet from the wreckage, had cuts on his face and a gash in his left leg. In those first moments, no one knew the nature of the collision. Three presidents had been assassinated since the Civil War, and the Secret Service was designed to protect this one. Roosevelt, as the story was recounted in the *Chicago Tribune*, confronted the motorman Luke Madden with his fist under the man's nose. "If your car got out of control. If it got away from you, why, then, that is one thing. But if it is anything else this is a damnable outrage," he cursed, his voice and body shaking.[19]

Satisfied that the collision was not an attempted assassination, the president went on to the Curtis House in Lenox, where he had been scheduled to speak. "We have had a sad accident," he told the group that had gathered. "One of our party, a faithful friend, has been killed, and our driver hurt, probably fatally. You will easily understand that under the circumstances I cannot speak to you, much as I appreciate your kindness in greeting me." Edith Wharton, who lived nearby, stood with the group on the lawn and later wrote to Sara Norton, "I think if you could have seen